D1378250

Ellen,
my dear, a
joy to share with
Merle's daughter —
Read, laugh + have a party!

My love, God Bless,
Pauline Scott

Drawings by JOHN KOLLOCK

IT'S FUN
TO
ENTERTAIN

A Humorous
Factual
Creative
Guide
to Entertaining

Blackie Scott

PEACHTREE PUBLISHERS, LTD.

Published by
PEACHTREE PUBLISHERS, LTD.
494 Armour Circle, N.E.
Atlanta, Georgia 30324

Copyright © 1983 Blackie Scott

All rights reserved. No part of this book may be
reproduced in any form or by any means without
the prior written permission of the Publisher,
excepting brief quotes used in connection with
reviews, written specifically for inclusion in a
magazine or newspaper.

Manufactured in the United States of America

Tenth Printing (1993)

ISBN: 0-931948-42-8

Library of Congress Catalog Card Number 83-60340

to
My family
Jack, Suzanne, John, and, especially,
our Jamie and Emily

ACKNOWLEDGMENT

Many friends have encouraged me and supported me in the writing of this book, especially Joy Mallard, Betty Coleman, and Margaret Straub Neil. I am deeply grateful to each of you.

CONTENTS

Page

DECISION

From our very beginning, Americans have loved a party! We have enjoyed entertaining in every situation from wakes to hoedowns to quilting bees to weddings to christenings. I was speaking to a convention recently and a man from Australia said, "By Jove, I do believe you Southerners would do anything for a part-ee." And yet, today, I find that many, many people do not entertain. I wondered why; so I asked. I gave a big audience about seven reasons why people might not entertain. "Lack of confidence" and "Oh, my, it costs too much" brought the loudest applause. I hope that by the time you finish reading this book you will just be eager to have a party!

One of the greatest sermons I have ever heard was entitled, "With a Friend and Your Faith, You Can Do Anything," and I can assure you that entertaining is the time you really need a friend. Now, I don't mean your husband! Husbands tend to evaporate. You need to have that Good Friend who is going to be right there when you need her. If you don't now have that friend, then *you* become that friend, and you will.

Those of you who plan to have a perfect home—everything in its place, china service, crystal, linens in perfect order—will never have a party. In my own home I never clean before guests come. I tidy up; I may dust a bit, but never vacuum until they leave. I turn on the lamps, and if they are too bright, I change the bulbs until the light is soft. I always have some music, use a door decoration, and place a centerpiece on the dining table. (It doesn't have to be costly.) I have everything done ahead of time, so that I can be there to greet my guests and have a totally relaxed and fun time.

I have learned that eighty percent of all entertaining is done because we have to. "They're going to move out of town, and if we don't have a party soon, they will be gone." "The baby is going to be born; we must have a shower." "The wedding is going to be in a month, and we must entertain." "John got a promotion, and we must . . . " Let's take the holiday season, for instance. The dates of Thanksgiving and Christmas have never changed and we are always ready! So my advice first is to say, "I *will* entertain," and either get that invitation in the mail or make that phone call. All of us perform better under pressure. So once the invitation has been extended, your little coattail will be straight out, for, my dear, you are going to have a party!

As I write, I am looking at a lovely piece of cross-stitch that was done by a precious friend, and it says, "Dust is a protective covering for furniture." Now, that was not given to me accidentally. When I entertain, my bed is usually unmade; I have to have a "take-to room." As I am scurrying through the house, I say, "Take this to the bedroom and close the door." Most of my formal dinner parties have been given with an unmade bed behind a door that is closed and sealed with masking tape! So, if you can accept the fact that you cannot do *everything*, you will entertain more often, you will gain confidence each time you entertain, and you will have fun.

There are four general rules for food if you want to enjoy your guests: 1. Have something that may be kept in the kitchen after the guests arrive (chicken divan or stroganoff); 2. Plan something you can make ahead of time (frozen salad, marinated vegetables) and turn your back on in the kitchen while you greet your guests; 3. Have something inexpensive enough so that you can feed a lot of guests without its costing you an arm and a leg; 4. And, of course, make it delicious, especially good. Some part of the meal should be outstanding. Develop specialties of your own—your guests never have your stroganoff except at your house. And please be sure that you try out recipes first on your family; perfect them before you serve a new dish to your guests.

One young cook's sad experience illustrates the importance of this precaution. I was called by a sweet young thing, the wife of an executive, whose guests were very influential in her husband's business. When I entered the kitchen and we surveyed a large pot of Creole seafood, bubbling, she asked me, "How does it look to you?"

My reply was, "How does it usually look? Is it supposed to be thick or thin?"

"I don't know; I've never prepared it before."

There must have been at least fifty dollars' worth of ingredients in that pot—wine, shrimp, scallops, and who-knows-what else. She had already decided that it was not thick enough and had dumped in some old, shelf-worn rice. In attendance were black specks she couldn't identify. With that much invested in the pot already, the clock ticking closer to the dinner hour, there was no way we could start over, weevils or not. Quietly, I picked up a pepper grinder and gave a generous twist over the pot. Many black specks now joined the unidentified ones. "I may have been a little too heavy with that fresh pepper," I said firmly, "but I think it needs a little more seasoning."

Decision

There are going to be catastrophes, but there will be fewer if you have planned well in advance, know your recipe, keep your cool, and have a sense of humor.

Your entertaining does not have to be elaborate. There is a little doll on the market now that is not any more attractive or any more appealing than any other doll, but it has been presented and marketed with such a flair that it is popular all over the United States. The young man who created this doll has made millions! The same goes for entertaining. As long as we do everything with sincere interest in our guests, with confidence, and with a flair, we can pull it off! I can assure you that no one will enjoy the party any more than you will, and your guests will appreciate your creativity.

Fragrances are so important to all parties. Sometimes I call them mood setters. When you walk into a home for a brunch or a coffee, the first things that greet you are those welcoming fragrances. This idea was embedded in my mind when, as a young bride in Virginia, I was trying to sell a house. Someone told me I needed to give the impression that this was a warm, cozy, comfortable home.

Now, those who know me, know that I cannot sew a stitch—I cannot even sew on a button—but I got some needles and yarn and laid them on a chair in the den and put out some homey magazines—*Better Homes and Gardens* and *Good Housekeeping*. Then I put a pot on the stove to boil, and in that pot I threw some cinnamon, and when the prospective buyer walked in that cozy little house with that delicious aroma wafting throughout, I can tell you that it did make a difference. They bought that house! (The new occupants thought ownership made them instant cooks and seamstresses.)

So it could be with your party. You can really set the mood, by using cinnamon anytime, or bayberry fragrances at Christmas, or crushed coffee beans sprinkled on a centerpiece for a brunch or a coffee. You decide the mood you want.

I never wait until the end of the week to do everything if I am entertaining over the weekend. I jokingly say that we dust the plates on Wednesday because I always set my table on Sunday afternoon or evening. (I couldn't do this without the convenience of a separate dining room.) It is so helpful to get the table setting out of the way. I keep in mind the kind of party I am having, so that I can plan the door decoration and other preparations as I go along. I do check my linens early in the week. In these days of wash-and-wear they usually aren't any problem, but if something does have to be laundered, I have time. Then I check the house for the basics I might need for the heavier cooking at the end of the week. There is a frozen fruit salad that I always keep in the freezer. I urge you: don't go to bed tonight until you have a frozen fruit salad in your freezer. It is just wonderful! It is nice to put the salad into muffin tins (or baking cups) to harden and then pop them into a plastic bag. They can be used for a quick luncheon, for a formal dinner on a salad plate, or even on a tray to be served for a buffet. A tray is especially nice to have on hand to take to a sick friend.

If you are having a buffet, or a tea, or a coffee, place every container you plan to use where you want it to be. On a slip of paper, write the name of the food that should go into that dish and where you want it placed. Then, put the paper in the container. At the last minute, when Good Friend is helping you, it is so easy for her to know what goes where. I remember an occasion when the slips of paper were exchanged before a large buffet. Good Friend was holding a relish tray with a ham label and said, "I don't know how I can get all this ham on this little tray."

It is very important to have an empty dishwasher when you are entertaining. If the dishes in the dishwasher are dirty, put them in a pan on the back porch or under a tree outside, or on top of

Decision

the washing machine, but get them out of the way and out of sight. You need a safe place to put the dishes as you clean off the table—this is the most likely time for breakage. I always put plates in the dishwasher between the dinner and dessert courses.

The most important thing you can do the week of the party is to make lists and carry them with you all week. Perry Como sings, "I get letters, lots and lots of letters." You should sing, "I make lists, lots and lots of lists." (And you may even need a list of your lists.)

Start your master list as you check your inventory of linens, crystal, china, silver, candles, flowers (fresh or silk), groceries, menu, and recipes. It is absolute suicide to attempt to shop for everything you need in one excursion. Some staples may be purchased weeks in advance to soften the blow to your checking account. The very thought of leaving all the shopping to one day will exhaust and overwhelm you, and your checkbook will go into cardiac arrest.

Make a list of chores by days—what day to clean the dining room and living room and bathroom and kitchen (if you simply have to clean); what day to buy ahead-of-time staples, and what day to buy fresh produce and meats; what day to do your nails and go to the beauty shop; what day to set the table(s); what day to cook ahead-of-time recipes, and day-of recipes; and, of course, other jobs as you identify them.

Make a list around your menu, including recipes, oven temperatures, and cooking times (you may need to do some shuffling in the oven). You need a day-of time list—when to get out what casserole to thaw and, then, when to put it in the oven; when to take out the rolls; make tea or coffee; when to chop or thaw or mix the salad; when to let the wine breathe; and then, about an hour before guests are due to arrive, check your list with husband and Good Friend. (Two heads are still better than one.)

You should have time to take a long soak in the bathtub, including lemons on the elbows and cucumbers on the eyelids! Start early making lists and work from them. And now, don't procrastinate. It's fun to entertain!

Decision

INVITATIONS

Every person needs a calendar. Have a calendar with large squares, and your husband will love you, your children will love you, and life becomes easier. When I receive an invitation, I go directly to my calendar, write down the name, place, address—if I need to respond by mail, everything I need—and many times I tear up the invitation because it's all on my calendar. Party invitations should be mailed ten days before the event (or telephoned a week ahead). I check my calendar and respond either by telephone or by letter. It is normal for us to want to invite prominent people well ahead of time, but it is inconsiderate to tie them up for months for our party. Send all invitations at the same time.

In responding to invitations, you should reply in the style of the invitation. If it has R.S.V.P. and includes a telephone number, reply by phoning; if it has R.S.V.P. only, write a note; if it is a formal third-person invitation, respond in the third person.

Personally, I dislike "Regrets Only" because I know the social habits of people. Unfortunately, many people do not respond to invitations. To be sure of the number of people coming to your party, you can use "Please Reply by June 1," and then, when you haven't gotten a reply, it is appropriate to pick up the phone two days before the party and say, "Mary, this is Blackie. I have not heard from you and you know how the mail is!" (Isn't it marvelous to have something to blame it on!) If you have used "Regrets Only," you really can't call.

Urge your young people to respond to invitations. A party is a gift; an invitation is a gift, and you *must* respond. The example you set by responding to invitations is the way your children will respond later.

OUT-OF-TOWN GUESTS

It is always delightful to entertain out-of-town guests for several days. If you plan to entertain them by inviting some of your local friends to meet them, let me urge you to do that on the first evening they arrive. While they are truckin' on down the highway, you can be busy getting your house in order: the table set, the food ready, etc. It can be downhill all the rest of their visit, but on that first evening everything should be perfect.

I greet my guests at the door, show them to their room, and hang up their clothes in the closet, but ask them not to unpack their bags until after the party.

You do not have to have everyone for dinner; invite some of your friends for a dessert party after dinner. This is a fun and easy way to get a lot of friends together.

So, the first reason to entertain out-of-town guests on their first evening is that everything can be in apple-pie order, you are rested, and everything is as perfect as it will be during the visit.

Second, sometimes you are not really sure just how long your out-of-town guests plan to stay! So, again, Good Friend comes to the rescue. You can say to Friend, "I have no idea how long they are going to be here." Friend can come in and say to them, "I am delighted to meet you. Blackie has spoken of you so often. How long do you plan to stay?" And usually they will say, "Oh, we need to leave Tuesday—we must be back at work on Wednesday." Then Friend can report back to you, and you know that you will have time to take them antique shopping or to the lake, and that you are going to have to use that frozen lasagna, and your whole schedule will fall into place. Menus, activities, the entire week can be definite.

If you entertain on the first night, your friends can help later in the visit. While your friends are enjoying your out-of-town guests, one of them will come to you and say, "Oh, I just love your sister. She is such a dear. I do hope we can get together sometime while she is here." Do not bat an eye. Do not even breathe. Say, "When?" She may be at a loss for words temporarily, but usually she will say, "Well, oh, uh, would you like to come by for coffee on Tuesday?" or "I have tickets to the theater that we would love to share with your guests." Your house guests will enjoy this special time, and you can have a breather for food preparation, laundry, etc. We frequently have guests from other countries and it is such a wonderful opportunity for them to see the inside of more than one home. Most Europeans think all American homes look like those in "Bonanza" or "Dallas."

Out-of-Town Guests

RIBBON AND
DOOR WREATHS

Straw wreaths are just wonderful. Select ribbon of a color that is appropriate for your home, and buy an entire roll. Purchase a straw wreath and wrap it, creating alternate stripes of ribbon and straw. Finish off with a bow. Part of the ribbon can be used in making a corsage for the honoree. You can also use the ribbon to decorate around the house.

I have a green plant that hasn't been well for years, and I have a big, old fluffy bow on a little stick. When party time comes, I pop that bow in the plant container. It's like a transfusion—the little darling looks like it has come to life! In the winter months, when I do not have a lot of fresh flowers, I will use ribbon bows as a garnish on food trays or as a decoration around a candle.

I usually have greenery in my bathroom and, on occasion, I have used a bit of the same ribbon there. When you buy an entire roll of ribbon, all you lose is the little piece you put on the corsage. You are actually tying everything together with the same color—it takes so little effort to have a very festive party. The ribbon can be used over and over.

Wreaths that I use when I speak on entertaining are charming, inexpensive, and effective. With the following, and a little imagination, you can create your own wreaths.

1. Recipe Shower or Kitchen Shower: measuring cups, measuring spoons, rolling pin, any small kitchen implement on a wreath or a wicker mat.
2. Spice Shower: regular size containers of the most-used spices, tied by the same ribbon in which wreath is wrapped.
3. Redeye Gravy Party, Western or Tacky Party: red bandana, scarecrow stick-man, miniature tin cup.
4. Baby Shower: pink and blue ribbon; miniatures of bottles, rattles, booties; baby pictures of future Mom and Dad, weather-protected (inside of door).
5. Grandmother Party (party to honor new grandchild): doll with birth announcement.
6. Wine and Cheese Party: plastic champagne glasses crossed, with grapes, burgandy ribbon, invitation.
7. Bridal Shower or Luncheon: white ribbon, doves, birds, flowers, wedding bells.
8. Children's Party: clown, train, doll, ball and glove miniatures.
9. Welcome: flowers with ribbon, big welcome sign including honoree's name.
10. Easter Season: flowers, colored eggs (foam or plastic).
11. May Day: flowers, blue birds.
12. Luncheon for a seamstress: yarn, needles, measuring tape, anything that is a special interest of honoree.
13. Birthday for an older friend: something important to honoree, personalize with invitation or honoree's name.

Ribbon and Door Wreaths

FRIENDSHIP
MULTIPLIES
OUR JOYS

SHOWERS

Start with a theme that you can express in door decoration, table centerpiece, corsage, menu, entertainment, and all preparations. I like to attach a miniature object, such as a cup and saucer for a coffee, or a rolling pin for a recipe shower, that suggests the theme. The many fascinating miniatures available today make it simple and fun to add interest to the corsage and to the door decoration.

The corsage can be one small flower. You just want to say, "Here is the honoree." Once for a bride's corsage at a shower, I used a tiny coffee grinder that was later a Christmas tree ornament. I have also used a miniature rolling pin with the date of the party on it. There is method to my madness, you see! In years to come, as they look at that dear little ornament each Christmas, I hope they will say, "My, my, we really ought to go see Mrs. Scott in the nursing home!" (And if you are not now giving your own children a tree ornament every year, you should start. Otherwise, when they marry and move away, there will be one naked tree, and it won't be theirs!)

Select a chair for your honoree, pin the corsage on that chair, and under the chair put a folded trash bag, scissors, and tape, so that when the gifts are opened you have everything right there. Have a pencil and paper for someone to record the gifts. Everything is all together and you look totally in control, as though you give a shower every other day.

Personally, I dislike party games that require pencil and paper, and I don't think anyone enjoys them! Usually, I won't wear my glasses to parties for that reason—I can't play if I can't see. But it is nice to have some kind of entertainment. If the guest list is varied and everyone is not acquainted, ask each guest to explain her relationship to the honoree (friend, former classmate, old boyfriend's mother, sister). And, ask each person to relate some interesting story about the honoree, and to tell how long she has known her. It makes for good fun and laughter, as well as information. (For the groom, a wine and cheese party could honor him and stories can be in the form of toasts.)

As another suggestion, you might request in the invitation that everyone come prepared to give a household hint to the bride. Good Friend, with beautiful handwriting, will be on hand to record the hints in a book to give to the bride. This is interesting to everyone in attendance; yet it is not the kind of thing that requires pencil and paper.

Showers are festive and great fun. Use your own imagination, but here are a few suggestions:

Lingerie Shower: Guests should be friends of the bride—they know what type of lingerie she likes (a silhouette is nice for sizes).

Recipe Shower: Friends of the mother and mother-in-law could be invited. Good tried and true recipes are a foolproof way to begin showing off your culinary talents. (It would make a real

Showers

hit if you give dry ingredients for each recipe so the couple can stock the pantry.)

I-Couldn't-Keep-House-Without-It Shower: Guests bring the item they would most hate to be without, from silver polish to feather dusters to whatever.

Trim the Tree Shower: Fun any time of the year. Handmade ornaments are nice but not a must. Hostess can present small artificial tree as hostess gift.

Outdoor Shower (especially nice for the groom): This should be casual and, if possible, held outside. Gifts would be lawn tools, outdoor cooking items, house repair tools, etc.

Spice Shower: Great for young guests, who attend so many parties these days. Invitation reads: Jane—Cinnamon, Susan—Cloves, etc., including the most used spices and the rarer ones, depending on the number of guests invited. Hostess gives spice rack. This is a fun, easy, and inexpensive shower. Share recipes using your spice.

Linen Shower: Be sure to list bed size, colors in bedroom and bathroom. This is a nice mother-daughter party since linens are so costly.

Gadget Shower: Gifts come wrapped in paper bags, and honoree must first guess what is in the bag.

Wine and Cheese Shower: Great for a large group. Guests may bring a bottle of wine or a cordial stem to begin the cordial collection.

PARTIES FOR CHILDREN AND TEEN-AGERS

PARTIES FOR CHILDREN

All children love parties, either as a guest or as the honoree! I am amazed today at the number of men and women who say they have never had a birthday party. So if you plan a party for a child, go to the greatest lengths to make it just as festive as possible.

Encourage children at an early age to respond to gifts, particularly to those from out-of-town friends. Even before they can write, they can cut pictures of their gifts out of catalogs or magazines, paste the picture on the note paper, and, with your help, print their names. Mommy can help write the thank-you notes. With the same sort of encouragement, they can respond to invitations.

Many parents go to great expense hiring musicians, bringing in puppet shows, ponies, and all sorts of things. They are great, and the children have fun, but it really isn't necessary. Children enjoy a party so much more when they are participants, rather than spectators. A combination of both might be nice, if you prefer.

Again, the first thing is the invitation—phoned or mailed. The children could make the invitations themselves, using colored paper, crayons, magic markers, etc. The invitation could be followed up with a telephone call two or three days before the party. Children love receiving invitations! But note: It is very important, if the child is school age, not to send invitations to school unless the entire class is invited to the party. Mail them or hand-deliver them to the homes. And be specific about whether you want parents to stay.

I personally think that it is better that Johnny's mother does not stay. If Johnny is an active little boy without Mommy, he is going to be hyper with Mommy there. My suggestion would be to get a teen-age girl or boy to help you. (A large party could use both.)

Friend, with a station wagon, may return all of the children home at the same time. This way you don't have any stragglers waiting to be picked up, it's more fun for them to go together, and they don't feel that they have missed any part of the party.

The number of children to be invited should depend a great deal on the age of the child. My own grandchild had a birthday party and the guests were all adults. She was too young to enjoy another child, and grandmothers never like competition! A good general rule might be, invite two friends for the two-year-old, three for the three-year-old, and so forth until the child is around five or six years old and is accustomed to larger, organized groups.

A good time for a party for preschoolers is Saturday or a weekday afternoon, Saturday morning, or immediately after school for children six or older.

The door decoration should be a part of the theme. I love a hat;

children love hats. We become *that* person with a hat on. It is great fun if you can come up with a hat for each child. It's just amazing the way a little boy suddenly becomes an Indian when he has feathers around his head or an engineer when he puts on a cap.

Parties are such excitement that it is usually difficult to get the children to eat lunch before a party—so plan a mini-meal. Since little children love miniature anything, consider semi-small hotdogs, mini-hamburgers, individual pizzas, assorted shapes in small sizes of peanut butter sandwiches, etc. Follow with ice cream and cake, bite-size fruit, or a favorite food of your child's.

A creative and easy change from the traditional birthday cake is an arrangement of cupcakes in the shape of the numerical age. But, don't plan to serve from this arrangement. Light the candles in all of the cupcakes and let the honoree blow them out. Then give each child a cupcake from a trayful that has been set aside for them. Each guest will have his own new candle which he can blow out.

Butcher paper is one of the greatest things you can use for a tablecloth, and in fact, everything paper should be the order of the day. A fun game is to let the children draw faces to mark their places at the table. Before the children arrive, draw circles where you want them to sit, supply each child with primary colors, and give a prize for the best face. Write the name above each child's face; even if they cannot write, many youngsters can recognize their names when they are printed.

After many, many years, I have learned that children can feel rejected very early in their lives. When they are choosing teams at school and Tommy is chosen last or when he comes to a party and never wins a prize, the sensitive child will feel rejected. Therefore, arrange events creatively to assure that each child wins a prize. You might say, "We have a prize today for the little boy who has on red, white, and blue tennis shoes." Or "The little girl who has bows in her hair wins the next prize." Go through the entire group of guests and come up with interesting and unique reasons why each one won a prize. Then each child will go home feeling special because he or she won! It will be a real prize and not just a favor.

When my daughter was four, her favorite party was a dress-up party for her girlfriends. They came with their dolls, they wore Mother's hat and gloves and purse, tried to walk in Mother's high heels, and it was such a fun party! The parents enjoy the pictures taken at this kind of party—they are treasures.

When children reach the boisterous age, the best party is out of the house, unless you have a ver-ry large house. Be careful with your guest list; talk to your youngster about it, so that there will not be hurt feelings. At eleven or twelve years of age they enjoy scavenger hunts, skating parties, hayrides, patio parties, and "any excuse" parties.

A clown party is fun. There are some colorful paints on the market now that can be washed off easily like makeup. Use a clown on the front door, make hats out of crepe paper, and have Friend there to make up their faces. Everyone enjoys this! But be sure you have enough mirrors for them to see themselves. Borrow extra makeup mirrors. This keeps them busy and delighted. Then they can have refreshments and go outdoors to play any one of the games they are familiar with and enjoy.

Plan lots of outdoor parties. The children love the freedom and you will avoid cleanup.

Balloons are synonymous with parties—so always have balloons and plenty of them. Put them on the mailbox, on the chandelier, everywhere. Have enough to give each child a balloon when he leaves the party. They do pop and you are going to have unhappy children if they are distributed too soon.

PARTIES FOR TEEN-AGERS

My first concern with teen-agers' parties is that the host parents *must be at home*. I know that teen-agers are young ladies and gentlemen and that this suggestion is square and old-fashioned, but I seriously feel it puts too much responsibility on young people, if the parents are not present. Too many things can happen—things can be broken, there can be accidents, injuries, or emergencies—lots of unexpected things. So I urge you parents to be there.

Food for teen-agers is not difficult. Let them do their own thing: build their own hamburgers, tacos, or hot dogs; create their own tossed salads. Encourage teen-agers to prepare what they like, using their own creativity. And all teen-agers like dips and salty things. For dessert, the most popular choice is still ice cream. Here again, they can create a sundae, banana split, tin roof, or whatever. Make ice cream balls with a scoop ahead of time and freeze; serve in a large bowl. A big sheet cake is interesting, using an appealing design or the theme of the party.

Graduation is a special occasion and a festive time for the young people. Remember the colleges that they will be going to, and scatter about as many brochures and catalogs as you can. The door decoration is very easy. You can use the flags and colors of their high schools. A really fun thing to do is to have pictures of the teen-agers when they were younger. I ask mothers for their grammar school and junior high pictures, assuring them that the photographs will be returned. I secure these family photographs on a cork board, so that I can tell immediately if one is missing. Do not leave them loose, because they are treasures and the board idea works.

Spirit flags and other college or high school items can be used in the centerpiece. Music is wonderful—they always enjoy it. Learn how to "dim" the volume! It is chaos to put a large number of young people together unless you have some music and something interesting to stimulate their conversation.

They are high school graduates now, and I am going to leave their beverage up to you. By this time some of them may be drinking beer, and if this is all right with you, then that's fine. This is a personal thing between you and your child. Have cokes and other things on hand, too.

BUFFETS

The origin of the buffet is very interesting. Benjamin Franklin was our Ambassador to France between 1776 and 1785. While he was in Paris he was asked to give a Fourth of July party, and he was aghast. He lacked confidence, he lacked equipment, and he lacked the wherewithal to compete with the lavish Parisians. So he laid out his food on a long table and invited more guests than could possibly be seated. His guests ate standing up and overflowing from the house into the garden. Our Ambassador called this entertainment a "buffet supper."

When he came back to America, he said, "You know, it's the rage in Paris! Everyone is eating buffet." This spread to all parts of France, and years later the French designed a piece of furniture called the buffet, where the diner serves himself.

Today, every hostess has availed herself of this very practical and very flexible form of entertainment. There are so many reasons for entertaining with a buffet. One of the first is lack of space. You can invite as many guests as you can possibly get in all the rooms of the house. I go through my house and decide how many persons I can accommodate in the living room and in the den, and on occasion we have used even the bedroom. Thinking ahead is the answer.

If you cannot get everybody into one room, divide the most attractive guests, so there will be a quality party in all rooms. Leave a seat for yourself in one room and for your spouse in another. How many times have you been to a party and heard merry laughter down the hall while you were in a leftover group of three to five people? You really need to have structure in a buffet and you need to be in control at all times. Guests are more comfortable when they have been guided in a subtle way to where the hostess intends for them to sit.

Decide ahead of time whether you will serve iced tea, wine, water, or coffee. It is impossible to serve more than one beverage at a true buffet. (A modified buffet is a little different.) Go through the house and place a piece of stemware or cup and saucer at every place where you want a guest to sit: coffee table, side table, cocktail table, the hearth, etc. For an older person you may want to provide a TV table and set it in place after he or she is seated. To increase seating capacity, remove all of those lovely decorative pillows from the sofa and place them on the back of the sofa to allow for one more lady. (Now you know exactly where your guests will be seated. At a true buffet, guests serve their plates, then sit where the beverage container is placed.)

A buffet is a good mixer. We are so couple-oriented that we think we have to have an even number. It doesn't matter at a buffet whether your guests are couples or singles. I am especially considerate of the extra female because I feel that she should get just as much attention as the ever-desirable extra male. Guests can regroup themselves and mix and visit when they go back through the line for dessert. The style of self-service allows people to go around and greet others, and makes it possible for them to sit at different places for their dessert and coffee and to visit with different acquaintances.

You can use as many sets of china as you please at a buffet; they don't have to match. You may have eight place settings of fine china, ten in an everyday pattern, and Good Friend may lend you six. Flatware and stemware patterns can be mixed, too. So don't say you can't entertain because you don't have a complete set of china, crystal, or flatware.

And it's certainly better to use different cups and saucers than to rely on paper cups. No one has any respect for a paper cup! They will be left anywhere and everywhere, and a month later you may find one under the sofa. Coffee stains on the carpet are no fun.

A common complaint about buffets is that the plate is too small. Be sure to use a generous plate, large enough to hold entree, relish, vegetable, salad, bread, everything except the dessert.

A buffet is an occasion when you need chafing dishes or warmers to keep food hot between the first and second helpings, and people at buffets do go back!

You can make a charming, yet inexpensive, centerpiece by framing a bowl of flowers. Put a bowl of fresh flowers behind an old picture frame that you have carefully propped up on a buffet table or board. For effect, let some of the greenery spill over the edge of the frame.

When guests are coming through the buffet line, they will need both hands to help themselves to some dishes. Make an inset of bowls and serving containers, so that they will have room to put down their plates on the edge of the buffet serving tables. This arrangement may look awkward at first, but your guests will appreciate your thoughtfulness.

I would never serve spaghetti or a sloppy, loose green salad that

Buffets

might end up on the floor, or the guests. Select your menus carefully. For instance, men enjoy foods they can easily identify. If you have sauce or gravy, serve it separately and let them try it or leave it.

Remember that some recipes provide a smaller quantity than you might expect. And, invited guests may send regrets because of a conflict (out-of-town or unexpected guests) and decide later to come, bringing their "conflict" with them! This is time to "switch the spoons." Use smaller serving spoons and you can be assured that all of your guests will come through the line thinking that they have sufficient food, and if the food lasts, they can have a second helping. Or do you know about the versatility of pickled beets? It is amazing how they can fit in with any menu. They are colorful, delicious, and they do help fill up the plate. (You want the appearance of having the plate filled.) So when someone whom you may not have expected comes at the last minute, put the beets in your prettiest bowl and garnish with onion slices.

If you want to maintain a perfect plate with eye appeal, you might stand at the head of the buffet and, after assisting with the entree, add the garnish. Your guests will probably omit the garnish, but if you add this decorative touch, the plates will probably meet your expectations.

At a buffet, we usually try to serve only food that can be eaten with a fork, but you can provide a knife if you have something like ham. And let me introduce you now to my buffet "lapkin"! This is a large cloth napkin, as large as you can afford, used *with* a fine quality paper napkin. Fold so that there is a pocket to hold the silverware.

The first time you use the lapkin, you will have to show your guests exactly how it works: The lapkin (the cloth napkin) will go on the lap, with the plate on top; and the paper napkin serves the same function as the ordinary napkin you use when the lap is free. This idea is especially great for men! Men usually don't like buffets because the poor darlings don't have laps. However, a cloth napkin on the lap, holding the plate and protecting the clothing, and the paper napkin in the hand make buffet diners very comfortable.

There have been books and books written on napkin folds. I am always concerned when I see a table with these elaborate napkin folds, because I am sure the hostess spent the entire day folding napkins and I am afraid we won't have much for dinner that night. Really, the lapkin is such a quick, simple, practical, and easy thing, and it works like a charm. At Christmas time you can put a piece of ribbon around it and tuck in a candy cane; in the spring you can tuck in a fresh flower; at Easter, a bag of jelly beans, etc.

The lapkins do not need to be on the table. I like to put mine on a silver tray where they can be picked up after guests have filled their plates. Their filled plates and lapkins containing flatware are all they have to take to their seats.

Buffets are for those who have said they can't entertain because they don't have enough room. If you do not have a generous living room or dining room, pull out the trusty old ironing board, drop a colorful sheet over it, and then stack the plates on the end, next to the napkin packets (lapkins). The food can be served from the kitchen table, and guests can be seated throughout the house, including the bedroom. Clear the shelves of a bookcase for dessert and coffee cups. This arrangement will enable you to serve very efficiently, and the ironing board can be easily put away and the sheet folded.

The *modified buffet* is one in which you set your table, and as many card tables as needed, as you would for any formal meal. If card tables are used, each may have its own china, crystal, etc., and its own color scheme. Each table would be formally set with the complete place setting, including goblet, wine glass, salad plate, etc. As with any formal table setting, it is nice to have the goblets alike, but the wine glasses do not necessarily have to match the goblets. You may use a silver goblet with a crystal wine glass, or a crystal wine glass of one pattern with a goblet of another. Use candles, tablecloth, centerpiece, etc., as you would for a served dinner.

I always use place cards for more than four persons. (I have some beautiful porcelain ones that can be erased and used over and over.) Long before my guests arrive, I plan my seating arrangement and complete my place cards: If the guest of honor is a male, he is on my right and if it is a female, she is on my husband's right. I decide where to seat my left-handed people, and I intersperse the talkers and the quiet guests.

When I say, "Dinner is served," I have solved the problem of where each person should sit. In our home we have each guest go to his identified place, remain standing, hold hands, and say grace. Then each guest picks up his plate, goes through the buffet line, and returns to his assigned chair. This arrangement assures that the pink china will return to the pink table setting!

After dinner, avoid breaking the magic circle that may have developed around the table. Serve coffee and dessert right where you are, instead of moving to another room. You might put a cruet of a liqueur like kahlua or creme de cocoa on the table to serve in the coffee with dessert.

BRUNCHES,
COFFEES, TEAS

BRUNCHES

Brunches are among my very favorite parties. When I receive an invitation to a brunch, especially during the holiday season, I am absolutely delighted! We are all trying to sandwich in the company party, the neighborhood party, the Sunday school party. What a treat to be with our friends on a charming occasion that leaves an evening free! Besides, everyone comes to a brunch so rested! The friends who always seem to be late for evening parties—I don't know if they get behind every accident on the freeway or what happens—arrive for a brunch rested and on time.

The brunch hour may vary. Actually, you may have a brunch as early as ten o'clock. My family are church people and we find that a brunch menu is very agreeable after church. This is a good way to get away from that old pot roast and all of that heavy cooking. Serve something that is very, very easy. My favorite brunch menu is in the back of the book.

A great time for brunch is before a football game. Use a football helmet—old, real, or play. Get a chrysanthemum from the cut-rate florist, add a spirit flag of your favorite team, a few leaves, and presto! You've got a perfect centerpiece for a buffet.

Now, on Monday morning after the party, take this lovely arrangement to Aunt Minnie in the nursing home or to your neighbor whom you have neglected too long. You've had your theme and centerpiece for a tiny cost, and you have made someone happy.

The first rule for a brunch is never serve any food that has to be prepared the morning of the party. I could walk the Tallulah Gorge on a tightrope more easily than I could get poached eggs out of the pan onto that English muffin for an Eggs Benedict. I tried it one time and it was a catastrophe. A fruit offering is always important, usually a hot curried or spice fruit.

I suggest a cornucopia filled with pastries as a centerpiece for brunch. Buy day-old donuts; the freshness doesn't matter in a centerpiece. The donuts can be joined into clusters of three to five with toothpicks. I love those little donut holes. A centerpiece can be made as big or small as you like. I always try to add something fresh to each centerpiece—leaves or holly at Christmas, pyracantha berries in the fall.

Bring in your fresh clippings the night before and clean them. I assure you that if you bring them in on the day of your party, those little creatures that live in greenery are going to join the party. You will be embarrassed and your guests will be slapping at the little things hopping around the table!

COFFEES AND TEAS

A tea is a delightful way to entertain a large number of people. Sometimes we call a tea a reception when we are introducing or honoring somebody—a new neighbor, business associate, or bride. But, when the number of guests is small, we call it a tea.

With a large guest list, it is nice to stagger the time of the invitations so that you won't have too many people in the house at one time. The groups will overlap, but that is perfectly all right. You should allow one-and-one-half hours for each group.

This is the time to use your sterling silver service, if you have one, and a beautiful centerpiece. One of my favorites is a porcelain teapot with an arrangement of flowers that spill down into a teacup and saucer. You do not need many flowers. This is very easy to do. For something less formal it doesn't have to be porcelain—it can be ceramic or pottery. If the hours for the tea last until dusk, you may light candles.

Basically, the same fruit tray may be used for a tea, a coffee, or a wine and cheese party. Pineapple is such a wonderful fruit! You can divide the whole pineapple lengthwise, hull it, and put it end to end with toothpicks. Let strawberries spill over, fanfold red and yellow apples that have been cored but not peeled, and add grapes in clusters. This makes a beautiful, as well as a nourishing and delicious, tray. I clean ivy until it is shiny and line this tray with it totally so that the fruit will have a bed of greenery. Just before my guests come, I mist the ivy and fresh fruits. It makes the entire tray much more inviting.

A footed cake stand is such a wonderful serving piece. If you don't have a footed cake stand, beg, borrow, or steal one. A table is certainly dull if everything is on the same level. Put a birthday cake on a footed cake stand and it's an instant centerpiece.

Another thing I do with my dear little ivy leaves is to put them with fresh strawberries on the cake stand. Leave the stems on the strawberries for this, and serve powdered sugar or sour cream with a little bit of brown sugar for a dip.

You can use frosted grapes, either to eat or as a part of the centerpiece. If you are using them in a centerpiece, wash the grapes and leave them in a big bunch, roll in dry, green gelatin, and chill. If you are going to eat the frosted grapes, break them into small bunches and follow the same procedure. (This is much easier than the sugar and egg-white method.)

If you are serving sandwiches, put all of them on one tray, and serve all the sweet things on another tray. Mixed colors, sizes, and textures are pretty, and it is easier to replenish the tray. Always reserve a tray in the kitchen for replenishing the table trays. How many times have you seen people bring in a big plastic bowl or something that is terribly unattractive to replenish a tray? Ideally, you would have two similar trays, but if you have just one extra nice, simple tray, you can replenish everything easily. Good Friend can do this, leaving you free to circulate.

To create a delightful garnish for a sweet tray, pull a fresh flower through a slice of lemon or orange. Use parsley, radish roses, or cherry tomatoes to brighten up a sandwich tray. Add nuts, bonbons, or mints, and this is all you really need.

With a coffee, I usually try to have an alternate drink such as punch. In winter, hot cider or Russian tea is good. Many young people prefer Russian tea to coffee. Coffee Punch is another delightful beverage you can use in the morning or the afternoon during the hot months.

> *Iced Coffee Punch*
> 2 ounces instant coffee
> 1¾ cups sugar
> 1 pint boiling water
> dash of salt
> 2 teaspoons vanilla
>
> Mix ahead and refrigerate.

1 gallon cold milk
½ gallon vanilla ice cream
½ gallon fudge ice cream
½ cup rum

Add rum to coffee mixture. Start with half of the coffee mixture, add half of the milk and ice cream to punch bowl. To refill, add the other half of the ingredients. This recipe serves 50. Coffee Punch minimizes the choices at a coffee or tea and is so refreshing.

If the invitation is for a fairly formal tea, I would serve traditional tea, being sure to have sugar, cream, and lemon, as well as a sugar substitute. (It offers an excuse for them to eat that extra petit four!)

The British serve their tea in a very different way. They put about half an inch of milk in each cup before they add the tea. The lemon and sugar, a must for us, is optional for them. (They serve fish, cheese, sweetmeats—really a cold supper.)

At a coffee or tea you will need someone to pour. Plan to have a relief after the first hour.

At coffees, cocktail parties, or wine and cheese parties, etc., you have items that need to be hot. If you put them on a warming tray, they will dry out. I think it is better to have those things in the oven and bring them out fresh, progressively, letting that fragrance out as Good Friend circulates and says, "These are hot from the oven!" I use a piece of foil cut the same size as the linen liner in my bread tray which helps keep food hot and prevents stains on linens. If you put them all out at once, the latecomers might not get a sample.

One of my good friends has a recipe for a special spread for ham and cheese rolls. It is delicious, easy to prepare ahead of time, and can be frozen and then heated.

> *Ham and Cheese on Rolls* (for morning coffees or last-minute luncheons)
>
> Use any kind of small party roll (or larger rolls for wine and cheese party)
> Spread both sides of small rolls with this mixture:
>
> ¼ cup margarine
> 2 tablespoons horseradish mustard
> 2 tablespoons grated onion
> 2 tablespoons poppy seed
>
> Grate Swiss cheese on one side, shredded ham on other, and wrap in foil. Freeze. Bake until heated through. Serve "fresh from the oven" as you mingle with your guests.

When hosting a coffee or tea, please furnish a plate! A bread and butter plate or a salad plate is a suitable size. Your saucer is not large enough to accommodate your food and cup. This will give your guests much more freedom, cause them less embarrassment, and minimize the upkeep on your carpet.

I have pots and containers of various sizes and shapes—Mocha pots, after-dinner pots, pitchers—which I fill with greenery and little bits of ribbon and use throughout the house to carry out the theme. At a coffee, I make little arrangements with cups and saucers—one in the guest bathroom and another in the den. (You remember I can't put one in my bedroom because the door is sealed with tape!)

After the scene is set and everything is in order, stand back and look at the table. Does it have eye appeal? Is the color-coordination balanced? The overall appearance of your table is very important at a coffee or tea because the table stays "set" for the entire time of the party. Planning and working ahead will leave you time to survey your efforts, and Good Friend will know exactly how to be most helpful to you at the last minute.

Brunches, Coffees, Teas

WINE AND
CHEESE PARTY

A wine and cheese party is the easiest, most enjoyable kind of party I have ever given. Each year I speak to a number of large audiences in October and November. And I urge them, if they are planning a cocktail party during the holiday season, to change it to a wine and cheese party. It is just amazing how much easier it is, how economical it is, and how much fun you will have. For a wine and cheese party, I use a door decoration of two crossed, plastic champagne glasses, artificial grapes, a big burgundy bow, and I personalize it by making the invitation part of the design.

I decide on two wines. Now, understand, this is *not* a wine tasting party. A few years ago people drank red or rosé wine, but today almost two thirds will drink white wine. Keep this idea in mind when buying wine. I suggest a rosé and a nice Chablis or Rhine or Moselle wine. I buy wine by the gallon and keep it in the container, under the kitchen table out of view, with some ice around the bottles. My husband, too, has Good Friends, and we appoint two of them as wine stewards—a red wine steward and a white wine steward. They each have a funnel, they each have a decanter, and they replenish the decanter, using the funnel, from the gallon jugs under the kitchen table.

We must consider our friends who do not drink. Always have something non-alcoholic on hand. The new sparkling grape juice is delicious and can be served in the same stem you are using for wine.

After the guests arrive, my husband will usually walk through the group with the first tray of filled glasses. After everyone has a stem, my husband and I can then join the party. One of the reasons that a wine and cheese party is so successful is that the beverage source is moving, and that keeps the guests circulating throughout the living room into the dining room. Remember, with a stand-up party, such as wine and cheese, all chairs have been removed. Only the sofa and the stuffed pieces are left in the living room. Everything is arranged so that movement is as free as possible.

Fruit is very important in a wine and cheese party. At one end of the serving table, I place a large tray filled with a variety of fresh fruits, and I make it heavy with fruit! I put in as much fresh pineapple, whole strawberries, grapes, apple and pear slices as possible. Additional trays of fruit can be placed in the den or living room.

At the opposite end of the serving table I will have a tray of sliced cheeses—Switzer, Swiss, Havarti (each with labels on toothpicks so that guests will know what they are loving)—and thin slices of ham and/or beef. I mix mustard and mayonnaise, maybe add a little horseradish. (You don't really need a container of both; just mix it up and that's it—a good time saver.) On the side of the meat/cheese tray is party rye or pumpernickle.

I find that if I allow guests to make their own sandwiches, it takes very little time, they have exactly what they want, and they move on faster so that others can be served. I make sure that the tray is attractively garnished with radish roses, tomato roses, or parsley.

I use a salmon ball a lot. This is an easy recipe, something that can be done ahead of time.

Salmon Ball

    1 1-pound can red salmon
    1 8-ounce cream cheese, softened
    2 tablespoons lemon juice
    3 teaspoons grated onion
    2-3 teaspoons horseradish
    ½ teaspoon salt (plus a little more)
    dash Worcestershire and cayenne
    ¼ teaspoon liquid smoke (plus just a little more!)
    chopped pecans

    Drain salmon very well; remove skin and bones, flake; and set aside. Mix remainder of ingredients well and blend in flaked salmon. Chill and roll in chopped pecans. Makes one generous ball or two smaller balls or logs.

If I have some left over, I mold it and put it in the freezer to use later for a small gathering. I use a variety of crackers for the cheeses, but use a very plain cracker with the salmon ball. A cheese ball and toasted pecans served in a footed compote, complete the menu. Sometimes I do put a pecan dish in the living room. I do usually have a dip of some kind, but realize that "with dips come drips."

In my kitchen, just off from the dining room, I have a little spot where I place a dip; a side porch is another good place to use a dip. Use these "safe" locations so it will be easy to clean up afterwards. Some people hesitate to have parties because they hate the mess. It is easier for guests to wipe up something they have spilled on a porch or in the kitchen than to get it off the carpet. But think ahead, and your guests will appreciate it, and they will follow through.

I am not a smoker, but I keep ash trays on hand because I realize that I am going to have smokers. Considerate people go outside to smoke, but some ash trays should be available in the house. Candles burning in the rooms help with smoke and odors, but remember that candles give off a lot of heat. If you have a candle way down the hall in a family room or out on a porch, be sure you have someone who is keeping an eye on that candle.

You and your husband should be moving around. Try to speak with each guest, individually, for just a few minutes during the party. You have greeted them at the door, but chat briefly again—"That's a lovely dress." "How is Mary Sue?" "I understand your mother is not well." You really will not have time to visit at a large party.

A centerpiece for a wine and cheese party can be a very simple thing, easily put together. Arrange two bottles of wine attractively, fill in with fresh grapes and fresh ivy, and then as a focal point use some strawberries, or plums, or small apples, or cherries, or anything appealing to give color at the base. Here you are carrying out your theme. You may drink the bottles of wine later and you may eat the grapes and other fruits. (Grapes can be frozen very nicely.)

Concerning stemware, use glass or crystal. It doesn't have to be expensive, but do use a glass stem. I never trust those plastic stems; they spell catastrophe. You may need to borrow stems sometimes from Good Friend, and she may prefer that you do not wash her stems before returning them. Most breakage occurs with hand washing, and you would rather she did her own breaking anyway! Rinse her stems, but wash your glass stems in the dishwasher if you have one. (Fine crystal should be washed by hand.)

I tell the wine stewards to stop serving wine at 11:30 P.M. At this time, I offer coffee—real or decaffeinated, and a plain cake—usually a pound cake, poppyseed cake, sour cream cake, or any plain cake without an icing. I assure you that if your guests have a cup of coffee and some cake—usually, they will even eat some more fruit with the cake—when they leave, you can go to bed knowing they are going to arrive home safely. This is especially important during the holiday season. The afterglow of a party is undisturbed when you know your guests left your home in control.

The wine and cheese party can be extended into a full meal. The first course, wine and cheese, is heavier fare and could be set up in the living room or den. Proceed then to the dining room for soup and a green salad, followed by dessert. This same idea could become a progressive dinner, with successive courses being served in three or four different homes. It is a lovely way for friends to entertain together.

STAND . . .
AND
SMILE

PARTIES

ANNIVERSARY PARTY

Many people now are giving anniversary parties for parents, and I have been asked many times, "Tell me, how can the guests recognize the children, grandchildren, and all the other family members? Usually, it is a very large group, and we don't want to use name tags."

Here is a good suggestion. The mother could have on an orchid and the father, a boutonniere. Select carnations for all sons and daughters and their spouses and provide daisies for all the grandchildren. You can substitute any other flowers, just so they are all alike for each group. Now, the guests will have clues to everybody's identity. This is a very subtle, but nice, way to speed up recognition. Be sure to identify yourself to the honorees, if you have not seen them in a long time.

The sort of anniversary party you have may be determined by the number of guests you would like to invite. A reception or open house is best for a large gathering. This can be as simple or elaborate as you like. The cake is very much like a wedding cake, and I have even used the original "bride and groom" top after twenty-five or fifty years. This adds a nice sentimental touch. Punch and mints with the cake make a simple but quite adequate menu for an anniversary party. It is like a wedding reception; the food can be as lavish as the hostess desires.

Anniversary parties are usually held in the home of one of the children of the honored couple, in a fellowship hall or parlor of a church, or in a hotel or other public facility. It is inconsiderate to expect the guests of honor to host the party in their own home unless the circumstances are unusual.

If only a small family party is planned, a dinner is very popular. The expense can be shared by all the children. If all the children live out of town, a lovely restaurant is a perfect setting for this special occasion. Again, R.S.V.P. is a must. The honored couple want to know who will be coming and the hostess *must* know.

Gifts for anniversary parties should reflect the personalities, lifestyles, and activities of the honorees. Usually we think of gold or gold-rimmed gifts such as china or crystal for a fiftieth anniversary, but I have talked to so many honorees and they are interested in getting rid of, not adding to the things they have. A couple was asked at their fiftieth anniversary what gifts they would like. They smiled sweetly and said, "Give us a kiss and a hug; they don't have to be dusted."

A money tree for a trip is a perfect gift if it can be presented tastefully. A picture of the complete family of each child would be a treasured gift.

By all means, guests should honor the request "no gifts." But if you are hosting the party and some persons do bring gifts, take the gifts to the back room and open them later. Do not make this a part of the party.

A twenty-fifth or fiftieth anniversary party should be as elaborate as you can afford, a really special occasion. Sterling silver is certainly in order, a lavish bouquet, a lovely cake. Be sure to have a guest book and appoint someone to "encourage" signatures. People forget. And, seating should be available for older guests.

This is a wonderful time to have memories, and one way to protect them is with photographs. So do secure the services of a photographer; he doesn't have to be a professional. If you can get a picture of the honored couple when they were married twenty-five or fifty years before, it would add a lot of interesting conversation!

BON VOYAGE PARTIES

Bon voyage parties are delightful! A lot of people take cruises to Mexico, and Mexican parties are so much fun! Use a lot of colorful paper flowers; they are easy to make. Use luminaries to point the way to your house, or to the backyard; they are helpful as well as festive. To make a luminary, fill a brown paper bag with sand and insert a candle. Mexicans do this at Christmas time and it is a safe thing to do. You may have a friend who has a serape you might borrow.

Mexican food is different and festive. Tacos, for example, are easy to serve: set out the fixings and let each one help himself. Make your own tossed salad if you don't like Mexican salad. For dessert, a sherbert or custard is nice to soothe the taste buds after eating all the highly seasoned foods. (Better have plenty of water on hand, too.) This is a good theme party for friends going on a Mexican trip, and an easy way to entertain.

I have been amazed at the number of people going to Alaska! It would be most interesting to greet guests wearing a parka or fur coat. (Keep the house cold!) Ask a tour agent for interesting Alaskan posters. Make an igloo out of flour, salt, and water the way we used to make maps at school—mold it over an inverted mixing bowl, and use this for a centerpiece. Place the igloo in the middle of a piece of glass or mirror, outline the edges with sugar cubes interspersed with floating candles. Cotton batting might be used instead of the glass or mirror to look like snow. This is a very easy party and you are likely to have the occasion to give it.

APRIL FOOL'S PARTY (or Upside-Down Party)

You say you can't entertain? Here is a fantastic theme party that you will love, and you will wonder when it is over who had more fun, you or your guests. (You can use some of the same ideas for a Halloween party.) The flowers can be weeds; use garish tablecloths, all kinds of mismatched china, flatwear, and napkins; and play foolish games, and do something that really is in the spirit of April Fool's Day—surprise the honoree! Everything is totally unconventional. If you feel you have no expertise at all in party-giving but want to get some friends in, just call it an upside-down party and do anything your little heart desires. Invite guests to come dressed wrong-side-out; serve dessert first and entree last. Let your imagination go wild!

SECOND-TIME-'ROUND MARRIAGES (Parties and Gifts)

There is a virus going around called divorce. It leaves those of us who care for both persons in a state of wondering what to do. Here are two of my favorite parties for couples remarrying after death or divorce.

Have a wine and cheese party and ask couples or single guests to bring a piece of crystal stemware (not to be used for the party) as their gift to the new couple. This will contribute to their collection of lovely and interesting stems for their own parties.

Or, if you want to entertain the bride only, a morning coffee is nice. Ask each guest to bring a cup and saucer. The new bride will have a cup collection to show or to use for a large coffee or brunch.

Consider these suggestions for second weddings (for widowed or divorced): Anything with monograms is greatly appreciated, such as door knocker, towels, stationery with new name and address. The bedroom is a very personal and sensitive area. All new linens for the master bedroom is a must for most brides in second marriages. Depending on the ages of the couple, the other gifts could fill the usual needs of a couple beginning a life together.

Tips for any party:

* Have a "Plan B" you can put into action at the last minute to take care of any eventuality. If you are worried about rain, you would provide a coat rack on the backporch, carport, or some easily accessible place for wet raincoats and umbrellas. (Put wet umbrellas in the bathtub if you don't have an umbrella stand!) It is better to lay dry coats on the bed in a guestroom than to provide coat racks and hangers, unless you have a lot of space.

* Be sure your house is identified, either with balloons or a bow on the mailbox.

* Have pencil and paper available at the phone. Party

guests may answer the phone when the host is unavailable, and the phone won't stop ringing.

* When parking is a consideration, send a list of everyone invited to the party so guests can come together. It also saves embarrassment of guests calling friends to go together.

'TIS
THE
SEASON
HOLIDAY
ENTERTAINING

I love the holidays! One of my inspirational messages concerning Christmas begins with the thought that winter is a dreary time for all of us; it's cold, wet and difficult to get through. So wouldn't it be terrible to go from Thanksgiving to spring without the burst of excitement Christmas brings! With all of its color, sounds, fragrances, feelings, and meanings, it is one of the happiest times of the year. In the light of the true meaning of Christmas, we enjoy the togetherness of friends and family during these drab winter months.

Holiday time is when our traditions become very special. If you are a young family, establish some traditions in your own home. They will probably reflect the ones enjoyed in your own childhood. If there were no traditional ceremonies in your family, you can create one for your children. It doesn't take long with children—once is "nice"; second year it is "expected"; and by the third year, "Listen! at our house we *always* . . . !" Children love to anticipate the expected. I have a dear Jewish friend who said that after seeing *Fiddler on the Roof*, that wonderful play and movie, many of the younger generation who had previously ignored Jewish traditions had become aware of them and were adopting them.

Holiday Entertaining

When planning your holiday centerpiece, remember that for Easter or Thanksgiving, it really doesn't matter how fragile the centerpiece is. That little pilgrim's hand may not be on too securely, or the Easter eggs may roll at the slightest jar of the table, but that's all right; it's for only one meal. But the Christmas centerpiece has many more demands on its performance.

Consider these demands when you begin to plan your holiday entertaining early in December. Be sure the centerpiece is well constructed. Place it on a tray, board, or something substantial so that it can be moved on and off the table as you change linens, etc. If it is made of fresh greenery, be sure of the availability of the replacements. Fresh fruits are always available and should be replaced from time to time. (Store in cool place when not in use.)

Being a Virginian, I love the Williamsburg feeling—fresh greenery, fruits, nuts, pine cones, etc. Did you know that the pineapple is a symbol of hospitality? Legend has preserved the story of the origin of this symbolism. Ships sailed from Nantucket Island to the South Seas in search of whale oil. There sailors discovered a strange and exotic fruit never seen by North Americans—the pineapple. Sea captains would bring back this unusual fruit as a prized gift for their families and friends. Upon their return to Nantucket or Newport, they would place a pineapple over the spike on their iron gate. This was public notice that the captain had returned and was holding "Open House"—food and drink for all. Hence the pineapple has become our symbol of hospitality.

An apple cone (an apple "tree" with a pineapple on top) is a popular centerpiece. It is a delight on the dining table, but I prefer to put my apple cone on a chest in the foyer or on a side table, like a hunt board or harvest table. I like the hurricane globes and candles on the dining table at Christmas. I arrange them with a wreath of fresh greenery and nuts and/or fruits on a runner of velvet or felt. It is easier to have the protected candlelight, which the glass reflects beautifully.

You can create another simple but interesting arrangement by using a smaller cone with lemons or limes. I like to place this on the kitchen table or a small chest. It is pretty and adds a special fragrance in the kitchen. Try varigated pittosporum as the greenery with lemons or limes; it is elegant! A pair of these smaller cones on a long table with brass or silver candleholders is pretty. (Remember, we need four, or two pairs.) I am not a garden club arranger, so you may have a lot more expertise than I do.

Many of you who cannot be with real family should start a custom of joining another family in your same situation. This could be the beginning of a beautiful tradition with that special warmth that comes with expectation. Call them early and start making plans as soon as Halloween is over! Suddenly you have something very family-like to look forward to. The brunch is a nice occasion to share with close friends before things get too hectic or as a part of the family Christmas celebration.

A cookie exchange party is great fun, easy, and a delightful way to sample a lot of different cookies. Invited guests are asked to bring two or three or four dozen cookies—one dozen to be served at the party. If they bring three dozen cookies to the party, they take home two dozen different cookies or as much variety as is available. Guests might be asked to share the cookie recipes (optional). The hostess furnishes coffee or a hot wassail bowl. If you have a large home and shy away from parties, this is your party! The guests bring their offerings on trays ready to serve. This is a fun tradition you can start in your neighborhood.

Progressive parties can provide happy occasions any time of the year, but they are a perfect way for the gang to get together and share the joy of the holiday season. (I heard of one gal who moved when it was her turn to host the big Christmas party! She might still be living happily in her old home if she had discovered the progressive party.)

Most hostesses are comfortable with at least one course at Christmas and enjoy preparing it annually, as I do my coconut pie. Some groups may prefer to alternate courses every year. Give several couples the responsibility of providing the entree course so that it won't be a financial burden on one family. Young people love this kind of party, and it is a perfect time for them to accept the responsibility of hosting their own party.

When people begin talking about caroling in the condo, you know times have changed. People who live in condos can make the most of close neighbors by caroling together and winding up at the clubhouse for hot drinks. If friends and family are visiting, take them along, picking up new carolers as you go. Again, decide when you are going to sing, and make it a firm annual date.

People look forward to this sort of occasion and appreciate not having to make a commitment. If you do plan to "come along," share in the refreshments. This may start out as a very loose party, but, if repeated, can develop into a special tradition. Celebrants who play guitars might bring along their instruments for accompaniment.

WASH-AND-WEAR
VS.
IRONING BOARD
LINENS

L inens have a long history. They are noted in the Bible and we find various references to table coverings since the beginning of civilization. The rough tables in medieval England were covered with Turkish carpets, which were then draped with linen cloths.

The napkin has been in and out of usage. In sixteenth century England, napkins were generous in size and rectangular in shape. A French marquis noted in 1780 that napkins were not used and that one had to wipe his mouth on the tablecloth. Fifty years later, a manual for servants instructed: "Put on your napkin, having them neatly folded so as to admit the bread into them without being seen." During the 1800's, after the finger bowl was used and removed, the cloth was rolled up and taken away so that dessert and wine could be served on the bare table.

George Washington's table had the "layered look." Having visited the President, one of our Congressmen from New York wrote his wife in 1817, concerning his meal at Mt. Vernon: "We had a light and late breakfast and dined at four. The table was spread with double tablecloths." The top cloth was removed between courses; the last course, wine and fruits and nuts, was served on the bare table.

Today we use everything from a combination of cloths and place mats, down to the plain mahogany table. Although we do not remove a layer, it is acceptable to place mats over a cloth if the colors enhance the table setting.

The formal cloth has been replaced to some degree in our casual society by very lovely linen, silk, and lace place mats, which are placed on table runners. I do prefer a cloth when the table is being seated to capacity—every inch of space can be utilized with a cloth. I think too many mats look like a patchwork quilt. With fewer people at the table, I like mats because they leave great parts of the table uncovered and one can see the lovely expanse of wood.

Let's consider lengths of tablecloths. A buffet linen can drop sixteen to twenty-four inches or all the way to the floor. *All* tablecloths should have a minimum ten-inch drop. I usually use the middle-of-the-road (a twelve-to-fourteen-inch) drop.

You can layer a cloth if your buffet linen is not the correct length, but is the perfect color you want to coordinate your table. Use a longer cloth of a blending color, and then put the "perfect color" on top.

Most place mats are twelve to fourteen inches by sixteen to eighteen inches. However, napkins come in various sizes. Buffet napkins are eighteen to twenty-four inches; dinner napkins can be eighteen or twenty or twenty-two inches; tea napkins are twelve inches; and cocktail napkins are four to six inches. Most of us have two sizes only. With the convenience of wash-and-wear fabrics and the washer/dryer readily available, cloth napkins can be used daily; freshly-laundered napkins really add a quality to dining. For breakfast, use a different color napkin ring for each family member, and even for house guests. (Toss napkins in the washer after the second use.)

The greatest invention since the buffet is a lapkin. Books and books have been written on napkin folds, but the lapkin fold is easy and functional, and an arrangement of lapkins on a tray can be quite attractive. Fold a large cloth napkin (as large as you can afford) in half; then, fold that in half. Starting at the corners, count three layers and fold these down. Place a quality paper napkin inside the pocket that has been formed; then add fork and knife. Fold back the sides, tie loosely with ribbon, and place all lapkins together on a tray at the end of the buffet table.

Another simple fold for breakfast or for very casual dining is achieved by tying a loose knot in the napkin. This looks bright and cheerful on the table.

Napkin rings are making a fast comeback. They are as varied as our place settings; so select them to complement your linens, china, crystal, etc. For an easy, quick, holiday family ring, sew a 5½-by-1½-inch braid strip into a ring. This same braid could be part of your runner for a total effect. Runners can be crossed and used as placemats.

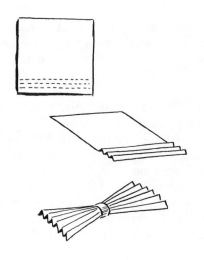

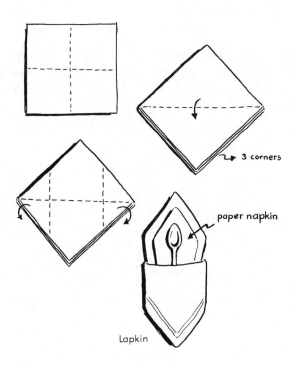

3 corners

paper napkin

Lapkin

CHINA, CRYSTAL, FLATWARE PLACEMENT

The daily routine of mealtime necessitates setting the table and then clearing the table. These tasks are usually allocated to children in the family—except when company's coming! Setting the table drastically changes from a simple procedure to a dramatic performance. The one who sets the table is second only in importance to the cook as she prepares the sauce that will caress the entree. Just a hint of lemon and a combination of secret spices make up the recipe that has been in the family for years. But the orchestration of the table will be visible for all to appreciate.

The reason for inviting guests to dinner is quite simple. You want to share your meal and enjoy their fellowship. Your table should be set in a manner that will enhance your time together. Many times I have toned down a setting if I felt my guests would be more comfortable in a simpler setting.

The following table settings have served me well and are flexible. They are correct, make sense, and are practical, and allow you to set your table with confidence and assurance.

China, Crystal, Flatware Placement

BREAKFAST

For breakfast, I usually use brightly colored place mats and napkins. If you do not have a napkin ring, use a simple, knotted fold in the napkin. I like the knotted napkin above the breakfast plate. The teaspoon can be on the saucer with the coffee cup. When I serve cereal, I always put the coffee spoon on the saucer; I use a bread and butter plate only when I have a full breakfast or have house guests.

Again, if you are crowding the table, a cloth does accommodate more people than place mats do.

A perfect centerpiece for breakfast is fresh fruit accented with fresh leaves. Acuba leaves are outstanding on a footed compote of lemons and limes. Shiny holly leaves on apples in crystal or silver or wooden bowls are very attractive, but it should be in keeping with your breakfast tone. White and brown eggs in chicken wire can be used for a hurry-up centerpiece. The beautiful copper colanders can be used very effectively with fresh vegetables and fruits.

Serve plates that have already been prepared for ladies' luncheons, especially on bridge day. Most bridge luncheons are the noon interruption to trumps and slams. For either an anytime buffet or a luncheon, I always use bread and butter plates. It is nice to have an attractive, molded butter on each plate. The plate can accommodate any relish that is served. If the luncheon is going to be the day's main meal, use individual salad plates with the same place setting as for an informal dinner. I tend to call this a true dinner at the luncheon hour. The evening meal after the theater or an outing could be a cold plate or something light. You might serve two meals a day when entertaining house guests: brunch and dinner in the evening.

Now for the drink. For a festive luncheon I like to serve champagne as the guests arrive. It can be taken to the table and enjoyed throughout the meal. Champagne can be served before, during, or after a meal. A person in my audience once asked, "When do I serve champagne?" You can always serve this wine at any hour and know it is correct. We Americans have used the saucer champagne stem, but Europeans have always preferred the tall, continental champagne stem. It seems that we, too, are adopting the tall stem, and it does enhance the flavor and contains the bubbles longer.

Ice tea or iced coffee is a perfect luncheon beverage. I usually serve coffee only with dessert. It is easier and I find that most of my guests enjoy coffee, and it affords me the opportunity to change the flavor, perhaps by adding a bit of cinnamon. I would hesitate to take this liberty if coffee were the main beverage for the meal. Also, many guests today refuse dessert, and they can have a "special" coffee while the others enjoy dessert.

If I ever use a fancy napkin fold, now is the hour! Napkins can serve as the needed color for your table if you are using your favorite green plant or any other decoration with a quiet color

China, Crystal, Flatware Placement

for your centerpiece. Many of you have a simple white china with gold or platinum bands which is lovely on colored cloths. I think a bold napkin in a softer tone of the same color as the cloth can really make a luncheon table outstanding. Place the napkin in the goblet only if you plan to pour the water after guests are seated. The butterfly fold used with a napkin ring allows me to fix the plates and pour the water before guests are seated.

The continental placing of the dessert flatware is always a timesaver and is so easy for us who entertain without assistance. This flatware would include the coffee spoon, a long iced beverage spoon for parfaits, fork for cake, pie, extra spoon for ice cream, sherbert, etc.

DINNER

Dinner is the masterpiece! Many of us today prefer the modified buffet, and I like it because my table can be truly beautiful, using candles, centerpiece, etc. (The food will be on the buffet for self-service.) The third wine is served only when a first course is served. The empty glass must be removed, and it is simple to do this, if you are removing a cover. Most of us prefer that the first course be served in another room in the form of hors d'oeuvres, even soup in a cup with bread sticks. There are many ways to enjoy an acceptable first course before being formally seated at the table.

The table will be set with the water goblet and wine glass in place—your preference of red or white wine. The knife is alone on the right, if a soup or fish or fruit cocktail is not served. The salad fork is almost *always* on the outside on the left if a salad course is served. It can be on the outside if your salad is vegetable or fruit or any food you would enjoy tasting first. We Americans serve so many sweet salads, frozen or gelatin, that I always put my salad fork on the inside, which gives my guests the liberty to taste their entree or vegetable first and then back to the sweet salad as the meal progresses. This is totally my preference, from having entertained so many Europeans who were confused with a dessert-type salad. I later found most Americans would prefer not to begin the meal with a sweet taste. I do use a bread tray, a butter dish, and relish tray on the table.

We have heard much said about a salt and pepper for each two persons. I find that one pair on either end of the table for six to eight guests is adequate. For a large table, you might use two pairs on each side.

If a soup or cocktail is not served, of course you would not display silver for them.

Whether serving from the table or in a modified buffet, I always have salad on the table. The entree is served by my husband, whom I always brief ahead of time. If your holiday turkey is out of a Norman Rockwell painting, dance through the house with

China, Crystal, Flatware Placement

it before carving to let your guests appreciate what is to come. If your husband is comfortable carving with all eyes upon him, that is fine; but, if he prefers, allow him to carve the bird in privacy. Bring the platter to the table with the meat cut into serving pieces; garnished with orange cups filled with sweet potato souffle, or crabapples, or fresh grapes, etc.

I usually have the other two vegetables at my end of the table and serve the guests if the dishes are too hot to be passed. We pass food from left to right.

For men, the cuisine is the most important factor. Be sure to have enough of at least one vegetable and a smaller serving of the entree for seconds.

I find it easier to serve the dessert at the dinner table. Also, when we disband I always find that someone will check the time and suggest that he must leave, and this automatically breaks up the dinner party. I do enjoy after-dinner drinks, after we have settled again in a more comfortable area.

If games or entertainment are planned, I think this is the perfect time. Many people dislike games, but some activity can be stimulating and can save a party if the conversation has not been very active during the dinner hour.

Singing is great, *if* you have at least one or two good voices. A musical instrument is helpful, and you should provide printed words. Someone's sharing a special experience is nice for all to enjoy.

Now it is getting late. The guest of honor does not have to be the first to leave. In the past it was considered incorrect for anyone to leave until the guest of honor left. Today we are much more flexible and realize that our lifestyles demand different patterns of conduct. If you must leave early, leave quietly. Give your gracious goodbye to your host and hostess and leave. Don't linger. They must get back to their other guests.

Another question: How can I encourage late-staying dinner guests to leave? I usually wait a reasonable length of time, get up and say, "It has been wonderful, but Jack and I must get started on our cleanup tasks. We will be glad for you to stay and help if you would like, but we must be up and out in the morning." My dear, they usually find their own coats and purses and are at the door waiting! Seriously, this can be handled in a humorous but firm manner.

If you are extremely tired, leave the hand washing of the crystal until another time. Put the food away, load the dishwasher, and take care of silver pieces. (Before putting food on the tray, I usually line my silver serving trays with a piece of clear wrap cut the exact size of the tray. Then the cleaning is easier.) Check your linens for stains and put them in the washing machine on soak. I use place mats often, and find that a piece of flannel cut one-half inch smaller than the place mat is a great insulation for my dining table.

Take down your door decoration and go to bed. You deserve a nice restful night.

China, Crystal, Flatware Placement

EXPERIENCED ENTERTAINING

AN AFTERNOON WITH JAMIE
(Grandmother Tea)

Most of my friends are grandparents and nothing is so exciting as sharing your grandchild's picture. But to have the grandchild in person is the ultimate!

If the grandchild lives out of the city, homecoming can be a very hectic time during at-home week, with friends and family dropping in at odd hours. So I decided I would have "An Afternoon With Jamie" as she visited the first time (three months old). Daughter Suzanne, Grandmother Blackie, and Guest of Honor Jamie were all dressed in best bib and tucker.

Our centerpiece was pink carnations, a gift from a friend. Silver baby cups, silver dumbbells, and baby spoons attached to pink streamer ribbons fell into place around the centerpiece. Pink punch was perfect for this tea; the petits fours' booties and monogrammed J's made the sweet tray "all Jamie." The door decoration was a doll, Amy from *Little Women* (used for Suzanne's ninth birthday party door decoration), in pink dress with more pink ribbons. Everything was finally in order and all who really wanted to share this child's presence, came! It was a perfect afternoon. (Jamie was a vocal, colicky baby, but she slept throughout the party!)

The big advantage of this kind of party, aside from the pride of showing off the grandchild, was that the rest of the week was free. The young mother could at last sleep late, as grandparents raced to Jamie's first peep. She could visit childhood friends and not feel trapped if Aunt Susie or former neighbors dropped in.

I have shared this idea many times and didn't realize how many of us there are out there! Grandmother teas are becoming very popular!

REDEYE GRAVY PARTY
(Country-Western Party)

My husband and I were the recipients of a country ham. This is a real favorite, and we thought, why not share this hot-biscuit-country-ham treat with friends? Brunch would not fit into our time frame; so we sent invitations which said, "Come Country - Come Western - Come Tacky - Come any way - But COME!!"

They did! They came in various states of country dress. We greeted each with our best Minnie Pearl "Howdy!" The last to arrive came attired very citified. We asked them why they didn't come dressed. With deliberation, they walked in and stated, "We are. We struck oil!"

Our door decoration was a scarecrow with burlap ribbon and the country invitation. A red-checkered tablecloth looked great with a centerpiece that was a collection of antique coffee grinder, butter mold, old metal syrup pitcher, all intertwined with just enough ivy and fresh flowers to get some garden club acceptance.

I was dressed in an old bonnet and a long dress with apron, and

I made biscuits in full view as part of the entertainment. I had prayed all day the baking powder was fresh. It was, because they did—Rise!

Our menu was eggs, country ham, spiced fruit, cheese grits, honey, jellies, and of course, those big fluffy biscuits. We greeted with Bloody Marys and ended with a cobbler and coffee. We all shared our best country stories. One guest, a well-known lawyer, told his tale of sawmilling and rafting timbers down the Altamaha River. Now his story was true, but I would hate to think the other stories were.

Relax! Have a red-eye gravy party one cold January evening. The cobwebs and dust can be part of the decoration!

WHO'S GOING TO DRIVE YOU TO THE DOCTOR?
(Luncheon for an Older Friend)

Be a friend to friends of all ages. I have been blessed with the caring of my daughter's friends as she lives in another city. I cherish the wise counsel of some of my older friends. It concerns me when I see people so hung up on age. To those people I say, "My dear, if all of your friends are your age, who will drive you to the doctor?"

Have a luncheon for an older person, your mother or someone else's mother, and make it special.

For your centerpiece find a picture of your guest of honor when she was young, in her teens or twenties, and place this in the center of the table. You might find other treasures of hers from that period of mesh evening bags or fans or intricate lace hankies—anything that has been special to her. Float a single flower in a saucer of champagne-sherbert in front of each guest. Tie a bit of ribbon from the place cards to the stemware. All conversation should be directed to the guest's interests—her church work, her charity work, how she met her husband, etc.

You can not imagine how this caring can change one's self-esteem. I received a letter from the recipient of such a party that said, "My daughter's friends have always thought of me as old, fat, arthritic, and cantankerous! Now they see me as an interesting person to be around."

Don't wait 'til birthday time. Plan that luncheon today. I will bet your honoree won't need nearly so many Bufferin for her numerous aches and pains, having been honored so thoughtfully.

THEY WILL EAT SAWDUST IF IT'S PRETTY (Ladies' Luncheon)

A ladies' luncheon is a special party! Now is the time you can experiment with all those fun recipes you have been waiting to try. It doesn't have to be a gourmet's delight; if it's attractive, ladies will eat sawdust! You might even call it a mystery luncheon to try out a new recipe.

So get out your prettiest china, crystal, linen; garnish the plate 'til it looks like a picture. The *oh*'s and *ah*'s will resound!

The centerpiece for a ladies luncheon can be anything you have and love. Do you collect small boxes, thimbles, salt and peppers, or frogs? Share your collection with your luncheon friends. You can display a small item effectively by turning a stem upside down and putting the collectable on the base. Arrange greenery such as ivy around the stems, tuck in a fresh flower or two (if fresh flowers are not available, silk ones will suffice), and presto! A *You* centerpiece.

You may have a friend who loves handwork and possibly shares her creations with you. Honor her on her birthday. Use brightly colored balls of yarn on a straw wreath, pop in knitting needles, and personalize it with a note or invitation, if one was sent. Display some of her handwork, such as a bit of crewel, or embroidery as a centerpiece. Put it over embroidery hoops, if appropriate, and add other sewing necessities such as thimbles, scissors, measuring tape, pins, etc. Again, work in fresh flowers and greenery in an artistic manner.

Put a needle with a short bit of colored thread in the corners of the place cards. Write the name of each guest in the same color ink as the thread.

I have a special friend that I need to give a really personalized party for. She has altered many outfits for me. I will buy anything that is a bargain, even three sizes too large. When I have indulged myself, I walk into her house sheepishly and say, "Friend, it needs only a tuck here and here and maybe one right here and . . ."

If you have a musical friend, you could give a charming luncheon for her. I arranged a centerpiece for a friend who was giving a luncheon after a voice recital. The table runner was sheet music, curled on opposite ends and singed on the edges. The tall candlesticks had musical notes dancing up and down (made from colorful pipe cleaners). Of course, the door decoration echoed the musical theme.

I always put the entire luncheon on the dinner plate. I never use salad plates, but always use bread and butter plates. This is an ideal time for iced tea with generous garnishes of lemon or lime. Have some mint? Maybe your neighbor or friend does.

A made-ahead dessert will cap off a delightful get-together. A bit of advice: Don't plan any other activity that day. Luncheon guests are like babies—they come and stay and stay and stay!

Have fun, share your treasures and your friends; make wonderful memories.

SURPRISE
FOR DINNER
(Basket Visit)

Many of you belong to organizations that may disband for the summer months. My suggestion is to keep in touch, or even organize some nice activity like a basket visit. Secure a market basket, large enough to hold a cake or pie or casserole, etc. List the visits the basket will make and length of stay in each kitchen. Make your specialty; call the next name on the list and tell her the basket will be in her kitchen on Friday with a chocolate pie (or whatever your specialty is). It will not stay longer than three days, and then she will call the next name on the list and pass it on. The list of names must be securely attached to the basket, and make sure everyone understands the procedure for taking the basket to the next recipient.

I shared this idea with a rural group who decided to put bits of news on the list. The first person to start the basket was the last to receive her "visit", but think of all the news she enjoyed!

Don't send the basket; deliver it and have a brief visit and share your specialty. If your group's treasury is low, you might add a money box (the predetermined amount specified on the basket).

At the end of the visits, you may not need to have that group garage sale to boost your financial standing. And, it was so much fun to keep in touch all summer!

COLD AND HARD
vs. HOT AND JUICY
(Family Suppers)

We tend to neglect the ones closest to us when it comes to entertaining. We use our fine china and crystal for company, and, I am afraid, company manners also accompany company table settings. Do begin early to encourage your children to learn good table manners. They do respond more easily if your table is set attractively. I don't mean daily, but often enough so that they will feel comfortable in any dining situation.

We often think the kitchen table is the warmest spot in our home. We all get together there for times of sharing and caring. "Did you know?" and "Guess what happened today!" introduce experiences that we love to hear about and will cherish. My favorite bit of philosophy from Kate Douglas Wiggins is, "Make a child happy today and you will make him happy twenty years hence by the memory of it."

I love candles. I think all of us over forty years of age do. (We look so much better in candlelight!) Candles are magical! Let me suggest a centerpiece: Fill a clear bowl with water, and, if you like, color it with food coloring (blue is my favorite), pour cooking oil over this, and float the disc-type candles. (The oil burns, not the wicks.) I surround this bowl with shells. Shells are ideal and your children are likely to have a collection handy. The centerpiece is so simple, made from things you have on hand. The candles are safe, for the water level is low and the bowl serves, like a lamp chimney, to keep the breeze from extinguishing the candle.

My dear, a cold, hard hamburger with all the family present—and even one candle—is much better than hot, juicy hamburgers eaten in shifts.

TIPS AND SUGGESTIONS

Don't apologize—if the food is burned, undercooked, late, or whatever. The most important thing is to ignore it. If you have forgotten a dish, don't mention it, unless it is the entree! Don't jump up and say, "Oh, I forgot. . . ." If it's too late in the meal, let it go, and forget it. They will never miss it, and if they do, it's still all right. Unless you forgot something on the stove and smoke is pouring through the closed door, handle it calmly with humor. "Laughter is God's hand on the shoulder of a troubled world." It is also very useful for a nervous hostess.

If you have a guest who is always late, tell him the party is going to be a half hour earlier. If he continues to be late, say, "Darling, just come for dessert." It is inconsiderate to the rest of your guests to hold up dinner for someone who is habitually late.

Iron monogrammed or embroidered tablecloths on the wrong side to bring out the design.

Do not stack glasses inside each other. If they have been stacked and have become stuck, don't try to pry them apart; they will surely break. Fill the inside glass with cold water, immerse the outer one in warm water, and the expansion of the outer glass will usually make it easy to separate them. Likewise, stack only one or two cups. A hanging rack is best, but cups can be protected with a paper towel or napkin between the cups.

Add ammonia to the water to bring out the sparkle in your crystal. Of course, it will need rinsing. Ammonia is also great for that added sparkle to bric-a-brac, vases, etc.

Don't wear rings when hand washing crystal or fine china. I ruined a priceless piece once, washing dishes while thoughtlessly wearing a large ring.

For china or crystal with gold bands that may tarnish, use a little silver polish to clean and brighten.

Fine crystal should never be washed in the dishwasher. The force of the water may chip it. Glass stems can be washed safely in the dishwasher.

Put rice and vinegar in the wine decanter to remove stains, and swish around. The rice acts as a mild abrasive. Small pebbles may be used if you are especially careful.

Most fine china can go into the dishwasher. It has been fired much higher than your water temperature. The damage to china comes from the harsh detergents (I recommend Cascade). If you are using Grandmother's hand-painted china, *do* hand wash—the next day when you are rested and at your leisure. I would just use that china for show! Serving on it involves too much responsibility for you and your guests.

Tips and Suggestions

If you have a tiny chip in your crystal, take a fine #00 emery board and, with a rotary motion, file down the chip, and run a little water over it. There are professionals who will repair crystal, but if the damage is minor you can repair it. When you have a party, use it yourself or give it to your husband. If your guests are due in fifteen minutes and you do not have extra stems, a quick repair is crucial.

If you don't have nice felted cases for storing fine china, use napkins or paper plates between the plates.

Except for knives, silver can safely be washed in the dishwasher. The dryer cycle loosens the knife handles after repeated washing. WARNING: If you like the rich patina (natural oxidation) on your silver, do not wash it in the dishwasher.

Salt or anything made of rubber will permanently damage your sterling silver. Do not cover silver with plastic wrap; this material will stick and permanently damage it. Do not store silver where it may be exposed to extreme heat, such as in an attic.

Most of us do love that nice stainless flatwear. Of course, discoloration can occur from buildup of detergents, etc., but it can be removed easily with a stainless or copper polish, or window cleaner.

Smoke is one of the worst tarnishing elements for silver. Line a drawer with tarnishproof fabric to keep silver completely covered. Actually, I don't want you to store all of your dinnerware and flatware, because I want you to use it often. Pet store owners have taught us a lot. They say that if you hold a puppy you will love it and usually will buy it. If you use something, you learn to love it, and then you will use it constantly! So I urge you to store it so that it will be safe, but do not store it so far away that you won't use it.

When using a chafing dish that has a double container, fill the bottom container with boiling water first. The food should be hot when placed over the boiling water.

Be sure to specify the kind of dress on invitations. It will save you from having people phone in asking, "Is it casual or what should I wear?" Specify on the invitation if you want them to dress casually, wear party clothes, costumes, or come tacky, etc.

When you are in charge of setting the tables for a very large church function or other organization dinner, write the name large on the front and back of a tent-style place card. When guests are from different locations, you might, for example, put "Atlanta Area." Then at least six persons know who you are and something about you. (This eliminates under-the-breath comments, "Who is the lady in the green dress?")

Music can set a mood. Low music is enjoyable and nice background for conversation. After guests have finished eating, they tend to be a little tranquilized; so, pick up the tempo of the music to enliven the group. Use louder music as guests first arrive and are a little ill at ease. They will have to speak louder and it will make them feel more comfortable.

To keep cold things cold without getting them water-logged, put cracked ice (not crushed) in a large clear plastic bag, express the air, and secure it. Then seat this in a large bowl or tray and cover with endive or parsley. Arrange cold foods on this bed of greenery. As the ice melts, it is contained in the plastic bag, the water is still cold, and the food is crisp and cold.

Tips and Suggestions

Never use just water for the ice mold in your punch bowl—as it melts, it dilutes the punch. You should freeze either ginger ale or fruit juices.

If your kitchen is small and you need extra counter space, pull out a drawer, set in a tray, push the drawer back to the edge of the tray. The tray sits firmly on top of the drawer, and is extra counter space. This is especially helpful when cleaning up after a meal.

If you have had a catastrophe (i.e., burned something) or have been painting and the odor lingers, sprinkle a few drops of perfume on the light bulbs. It is amazing how this scent will fill the air.

Candles will burn longer if you freeze them for about an hour before using. When you do not burn very much of a candle, use it again! Rub the candle with an old nylon stocking or soft cloth moistened with a little salad oil. I always try the wick ahead of time so that I won't have trouble lighting it at dinner.

If a candle is too large for the holder, let very hot water run over just the end for a few minutes. It will soften the candle and it will go easily into the holder. (I wrap masking tape around a too-small candle.)

Sometimes candle wax will stain tablecloths. Lift off as much wax as you can as quickly as you can. Place the stained portion between two pieces of clean paper towel and press a warm iron over it. Usually, the stain will come out. Treat wax stains on carpet/rug the same way. Scrape off excess wax, cover with several layers of paper towels, and carefully press with a warm iron.

Candle wax gets hard when it gets cold. So, if candlesticks (not wooden) get a lot of wax buildup, put them in the refrigerator until cold, and then flick off the wax. The remaining wax can be washed off with hot soapy water.

Wooden candlesticks would scratch if you tried to flick off the wax or scrape it off. Heat the wax with a hair dryer and wipe off with a paper towel. A mixture of vinegar and water should take care of any remaining wax. When completely dry, polish with wood polish or wax.

For interesting and inexpensive snacks, for teen-agers or the audiences of TV football games, add melted butter and grated parmesan cheese to a bowlful of popcorn. Great! Add raisins to salted peanuts.

Commercial Italian salad dressing is just wonderful. Pour it over asparagus or green beans for marinating, beef or chicken for marinating and/or cooking. One thing my son-in-law Alan likes is potatoes boiled whole, skins on, until not quite done. I slice them into thick slices, pour Italian dressing over them, leave them a little while, then brown on the grill. It is a delightful change from French fries and the old standby, baked potatoes.

Here's a steak tip I learned from someone in the meat business: cook steak to desired temperature, remove from grill, let stand for at least ten minutes before cutting, allowing juices to settle in again. It makes for a tastier steak.

Don't waste time icing petits fours! Cut a sheet cake on a rack, pour icing over, and let it go. After all, as my mother used to say, who will notice it on a galloping horse?!! They are going to be so delicious, no one will have time to examine every side to see if it is iced.

Tips and Suggestions

Use a fork to open English muffins and to make fluffy potatoes. For a baked potato, stick the fork—not the knife—into the potato, and twirl the fork around for a fluffier, nicer potato.

Bake or boil a large baking potato in the skin; slice, not quite all the way through (make slits), about every inch; brush with butter; sprinkle with grated cheese. Bake until the cheese melts. Delightful!

I am not a wok cook, but I have learned one thing: If you are cooking wok style, everything must be cut up ahead of time. You start cooking with a little oil, everything is twirling at the same time, and everything will be the same degree of crispness.

Use a scooped-out round loaf of bread as a dip container. Brush all surfaces lightly with butter and toast in the oven. What you scoop out can be used as bread crumbs; don't waste anything. A scooped-out cabbage is also a clever dip container.

Lemons are really a blessing to the cook. You can add lemon juice to cold water when preparing fresh vegetables and fruits to keep them from discoloring. Lemon shells can make interesting containers. After you have juiced lemon halves, save the halves (they can be frozen), clean out the membrane, cut off the bottom a little bit so that the shell will stand up straight, and fill it with cocktail sauce or seafood sauce or dressing for fresh fruit salad. If the lemon is large, you can fill it with sherbet for dessert or cottage cheese with a fruit plate, as you would an orange shell.

Lemon flowers make a great garnish for just about anything— fish dishes, meats, vegetables, sweets, etc. Cut thin strips of peel from a whole lemon, tip to tip, equally spaced. Slice the lemon in about ¼-inch slices, remove seeds, and garnish with the "flower" lemon slices.

When guests are late, holding food is always a problem. Remember to sprinkle a little bit of water over the top of a casserole or vegetable dish, and cover with aluminum foil. Sometimes we cover it with foil, but forget that little sprinkle of water. Do that, and lower the oven, to "put your meal on hold."

To serve dinner rolls or buns for hamburgers or hotdogs, place a rolled-up, moistened paper towel in one corner of the pan, cover pan tightly with foil, and warm in oven. It can be held hot several minutes after it comes out of the oven, and the moistened towel helps soften bread that may be a little dry.

Sometimes the dip trays get pretty messy. Under the dip bowl use a large paper doily which can be replaced as needed during the party.

Usually our dishcloth is saturated with warm water. To clean up flour spilled from baking, use cold water; it will not get nearly as sticky.

Never remove the caps first when cleaning strawberries. Gently wash in cold water, lift out, and remove caps after washing. Don't wash until ready to use.

To use up overripe fruit, mash in blender to use as a sauce for ice cream or cake, etc. Melons, bananas, strawberries, peaches, etc., are ideal.

Freshen up crackers and cereal by heating on a cookie sheet in a moderate warm oven for three to five minutes.

Butter the plastic wrap or waxed paper when you cover an iced cake.

Tips and Suggestions

Refrigerate paprika and cayenne pepper to keep out bugs.

Cornstarch has twice the thickening capability of flour.

For a nice, firm meringue, use one tablespoon of sugar for each egg white. I usually do not use cream of tartar. The secret is having the egg white at room temperature.

For a great drink for fall, heat together one quart of cider, one can of frozen lemonade, and a dash of cinnamon. Serve hot or cold.

Bananas become dark and soft in gelatin salads. Process the banana in the blender and add it to the gelatin mixture. The flavor is great, and it doesn't change the color of the salad.

Applesauce can be used as a lift on waffles, or add mint flavoring and food coloring to applesauce to complement pork.

To create instant patty shells, roll sliced bread flat, and cut out a circle; butter muffin tins, press bread in, and bake. This becomes instant shells for a special touch to such foods as scrambled eggs.

Sliced bananas in a footed stem with orange juice poured over makes a quick "company" breakfast first course. Garnish with a sprig of mint.

Milk, blood, egg, and meat juice stains should be removed as soon as possible with cold water; fruit juice stains need hot water.

Wine stains need salt rubbed in first, then hot water poured through the cloth.

Parsley keeps about a month in the refrigerator if you wash it in cold water, shake slightly to get most of the water off, and store in Tupperware.

For a perfect centerpiece for a card table for brunch or dinner, use flowers and a small taper in a cup and saucer. Insert taper into oasis in the bottom of the cup and fill in around it with flowers and/or greenery. It doesn't take up much room on the table.

Use terry cloth fingertip towels for family napkins.

A paper napkin liner in your wash-and-wear cloth napkin is a good way to protect against barbecue, fried chicken, etc. Someone asked me recently, "How do you get lipstick stains out of a napkin?" I jokingly answered, "Darlin', invite that person at Christmas when you are using red napkins." Seriously, I remove lipstick stains with a commercial liquid stain cleaner. I pour it directly on the stain, scrub the stain by hand, and then wash with hot, soapy water in the washing machine.

A brown paper bag is the best storage container for refrigerated mushrooms. The paper bag retains just the right amount of moisture.

Sift a little bit of flour in the processor when you are grating cheese to keep it from getting sticky.

Tips and Suggestions

SUGGESTIONS CONCERNING HOUSE GUESTS

For the Hostess:

1. Tell guests ahead of time what you have planned, so that they can bring appropriate attire.
2. Have an adequate night light; a strange room can be very confusing.
3. Have on hand and in view:
   tissues, extra toilet tissue, Bufferin, bland soap (for allergies), reading material in the bedroom, paper and pen near the phone for messages.
4. Clear closet space.
5. Fresh flowers in the guest bedroom. It's just nice!

For the Guest:

1. If you need a special pillow, bring it.
2. Ask before you raise the windows in your bedroom.
3. Encourage hostess to continue her routine.
4. Be flexible in your attitude and your food preference.
5. Never take a pet on a visit. Even a well-trained pet may not behave acceptably in strange surroundings.
6. A thank-you note and hostess gift is a must. After the visit, you can select more imaginatively.

Ben Franklin made a very wise statement: "House guests and fish smell after three days."

ETIQUETTE

Emily Post has been one of my favorite authorities on etiquette for a number of years, and now there is a book out entitled *The New Emily Post's Etiquette* written by Elizabeth Post, the wife of her grandson (Funk and Wagnalls Book , New York, 1975). I have been interested in the changes in our way of life—the way we dress, entertain, lifestyles, and Ms. Post deals with these new directions. We have released ourselves from the bonds of the "correct" thing to do, and, more and more, live in a way that expresses our individual personalities. We set our tables and serve our guests in a more creative style. This means we can do all of the interesting, fun things in our own way, and still be in good taste doing so.

Most of the entertaining we do in our homes today is informal, but there are some rules that Amy, Emily, Elizabeth, and I all agree on:

Always observe the hostess. If the hostess does not put her napkin in her lap when she sits down, the observant guest would know she is waiting to say grace as soon as everyone is seated.

Even if this is not your custom, you still follow your hostess's lead. (Ordinarily, you put your napkin in your lap as soon as everyone is seated.) A man should never tuck his napkin in his belt or collar. When the meal is finished or if you leave the table during the meal, put the napkin on the left side of your plate. If the plates have been removed and dessert is served in another room, then leave the napkin at the table.

At a dinner party, the hostess lays her napkin on the table as a signal that the meal is over; then the guests can lay their napkins on the table, but not before the hostess.

At a small table—two, four, or six people—you should wait to eat until the hostess starts eating. In a large dinner party, expecially a modified buffet, it is not necessary to wait until everyone has been served. Grace could be offered first, the food served, and guests then begin eating as soon as they are seated. A good hostess should be aware of her guests' comfort and say, "Please start your dinner. It will get cold if you wait for me."

Gravies can be put on the meat as it is served; pickles and jellies go beside the food they accompany. Loose nuts, radishes, and celery are on the bread and butter plate or on the salad plate. When you pass your plate to the head of the table for a second helping, leave the knife and fork on the plate but be sure they are far enough inside the edge not to topple off.

The host serves each plate and sends it around the table. The plates are started counterclockwise (that is, to the host's right). If there is a woman guest on the host's right, she keeps the first plate. He guides her by saying, "You may keep this plate." The second is passed on to the person at the end of the table; the third goes to the person to his left. When all the people on the host's right are served, the plates are sent down on the left side, and the host serves himself last. The hostess would serve in the same order, a male guest being on her right.

If you are refusing the food—because of allergies or diet—just say, "No, thank you." But it is good manners to take a little of everything that is offered to you. Another joy of a buffet is that you can help yourself only to those things that truly appeal to you.

In table settings, always place the silver from the outside in, in the order in which it will be used. Then there should never be any question about which piece of silver to use. You always start with the piece of silver that is farthest from the plate. When I was a Girl Scout leader, I tried to teach the girls that a teaspoon had a weak back—it could not stand alone. (A reminder not to leave the spoon in the cup or bowl.) If the dessert is served in a stem bowl or in a small, deep bowl on another plate, the dessert spoon is put down on the plate when you are finished. If the bowl is too shallow and wide, the spoon may be left in it, or on the plate beneath it. Likewise, the coffee spoon goes on the saucer.

I get a lot of questions about soups. You may serve either a clear soup or a thick soup in a cup with one handle or with handles on both sides. After you take a spoonful or two, and if it is cool enough, you may pick up the cup. Use both hands if the cup has two handles or continue to use your spoon if you prefer. (Sometimes old habits are hard to break.)

Clear soup is sometimes served in a shallow soup plate rather than a cup. If the level of the soup is so low that you must tip the bowl to avoid hitting the bottom and making a noise, lift the near edge in your left hand and tip the bowl away from you, and spoon the soup away from you. Be sure to leave the soup spoon on the plate under the soup bowl.

Bread should always be broken into moderate pieces with your fingers, not necessarily tiny pieces. Butter a small piece after you break it. Even the new Emily Post book says that hot biscuits and toast really should be buttered immediately, since they are more delicious when the butter is quickly and thoroughly melted.

Salad may be cut up into small pieces. The idea that this is incorrect probably came from the time when the salt and vinegar would ruin the blade of the knife. You shouldn't cut up a whole plateful at once, but you can use your knife to cut up portions of the salad. Many times a fork is just not adequate when you are trying to eat a salad.

The fashion of using mugs without saucers has created problems. Mugs are not proper on a formal table and are rarely seen on any table with a damask cloth. Use individual table mats on an informal table with mugs. The spoon may be wiped clean with the lips and laid on the mat or on the table beside the mug. The bowl of the spoon, face down, can be rested on the edge of the bread and butter plate or the dinner plate.

In 1904, at the World's Fair in St. Louis, a fine Englishman put ice in his tea—hence ice tea was born in America. A third of all tea drunk today in America is iced. This is not a formal drink, however; it should be served only at luncheon or for family meals.

Ice teaspoons may be left in the glass and held against the rim with the forefinger when drinking. That's awkward, but it's proper. The procedure mentioned above for removing the spoon and resting it on a plate is generally more comfortable. Our grandmothers had ice tea coasters with rests on them. The rests are rare items today, but coasters are available in many styles and designs and are so attractive. I urge you to have them accessible in the living room; don't hide them away somewhere and forget to use them.

Limp bacon should be eaten with a fork; crisp bacon may be eaten with fingers.

And yes, of course, Southern fried chicken may be eaten with your fingers! It is more comfortable to me to pull a piece into smaller pieces before eating it with fingers.

Cherry tomatoes are so popular and may be eaten with fingers, except when served in a salad or another dish. They do squirt; so try to select one small enough to put in your mouth whole. They are very difficult to cut.

Olives may be eaten with your fingers. Bite off the meat, but don't nibble around the stone. Remove the stone from your mouth with fingers. Bite a large stuffed olive in half. The only time you need to eat an olive with a fork is when it is in your salad.

Corn on the cob is something we enjoy and sometimes serve to guests. Avoid buttering all of the cob at once—don't be greedy. Take a moderate amount of butter, spread it across the whole length of two rows, add salt and pepper, then eat those, and repeat. Corn on the cob should not be served at a truly formal dinner party; it should be cut off the cob and creamed and buttered.

I am often asked about crackers. In the past, the rule was not to crumble crackers in chowder or soup. Now large saltine crackers may be broken and then, a few pieces at a time, crumbled up and scattered over the soup. Croutons are used a lot. They can be served separately in a dish or served in the soup.

Fruits with seeds—stewed cherries, prunes, etc.—are eaten

with a spoon. Put the entire fruit into your mouth, and when you have eaten the meat, you can drop the pit directly into the spoon and deposit it on the plate or saucer.

When most of the liquid is gone from your cocktail, it is acceptable to remove the garnish with your fingers—whether cherry, olive, orange slice, etc.—and eat it.

Shrimp as a first course presents one of the most difficult problems encountered by the diner. We are always told that we should eat shrimp in one bite, but if they are jumbo size, it is almost impossible. Grasp the cup firmly with the left hand, and cut the shrimp as neatly as possible with the end of the fork.

It is not necessary to leave the table to cough, sneeze, or blow your nose, unless it is a prolonged seizure. In that case, excuse yourself and go to the powder room. In an emergency, if you can't get your napkin or tissue to your face, your hand will do.

What if you see foreign matter in your food before you eat it—a worm on the lettuce or a fly in the soup? If it is not too upsetting, just remove it quietly without calling attention to it, and go ahead and eat. Sometimes that is difficult to do, but it really is best!

Toothpicks should not be used at the table, and certainly you should not pick at food in your teeth. If it is actually hurting you, excuse yourself and go to the powder room.

What do you do if you spill jelly or a bit of vegetable or something on the table? Pick up as much as you can neatly with a clean spoon or the blade of your knife, whichever is clean. If it has caused a stain, dab a little water from your glass on it with a corner of your napkin. Quietly apologize to your hostess, and she will probably say nothing because she certainly would not add to your embarrassment.

It is thoughtful to seat a left-handed diner at a corner so that his left arm will not bump into the right arm of the person beside him.

Candles for a very formal dinner should be white or off-white and should be new. However, we may entertain formally with coordinating colors that are pleasing to the eye and still be in good taste.

Candles are lighted before guests come to the table and remain lighted until they leave the dining room. The centerpiece may have a pair of candlesticks placed at each end. Four is the minimum number of candles for a table of six or more, but at a small table set for two or four people, two candlesticks are adequate. If candles alone light the table, you should count on a candle for each person. Most of us do use some artificial lighting controlled by a dimmer along with candles. The candles are actually adding to the lighting and are not merely ornaments.

All candlesticks do not have to match. I divide each pair, so that I have one of each kind at each end of the table.

Candles that float are so very safe, and they are fun to use in so many different ways. Simple in design, they are small plastic discs with a center wick extending above, and below into a layer of cooking oil that you have floating on the water. As the oil is burned up, the water automatically extinguishes the flame. Wax candles burning all over the house at Christmas time can be a real hazard, but floating candles are much safer and are very attractive.

Etiquette

Candlesticks with candles in them may be used on the luncheon table as part of the decoration, but they should not be lighted during daylight hours. A few years ago the rule was never to put a candlestick on the table unless it was lighted. So this is new.

I have been asked so many times about obligations. Weddings, showers, invitations to dances, or official functions, carry no obligation. Parties in a private home, whether luncheon, brunch, or dinner, do require a return invitation. You do not necessarily have to pay back an invitation in kind. If I have invited you to a brunch, you could return it with a dessert party.

If only one person takes a second helping, a considerate hostess will take a little, too.

When you have invited dinner guests, and an unexpected caller drops in just as you are having dessert, invite him to have a cup of coffee. Your obligation is to your invited guests.

Likewise, if guests arrive uninvited when you have other plans, you should say so. Your first obligation is to the people with whom you have made plans. There possibly could be exceptions to this rule. If an old friend comes in from out of town without warning, you may have to get in touch with your host and work it out.

Guests who have not cleared their intentions with the hostess beforehand, should never be hurt when their gift—such as cake, dessert, etc.—is not served at dinner. The same applies to a gift of wine. If it goes with your menu and if you do not have another beverage planned or another wine chilled, serve it. Otherwise, thank the donor and tell him how much you will enjoy his gift at another meal.

We are becoming so very casual in our greetings. Total strangers call each other by their first names. But there are a few times when first names may not be acceptable except by specific request. A superior in one's business should not be called by the first name unless it is obviously the office custom. A new employee, business client, or customer should observe what others are doing.

Professional people offering you services, such as a doctor or lawyer, who are not personal friends, should not be addressed on a first-name basis until they say, "Call me Bob." Most older people like to be called by first names, but I think one should wait until they suggest it.

The custom of calling family friends "Aunt" and "Uncle" when no relationship exists has generally gone out of style. This is still very common in the South, however. Sometimes our children refer to our closest personal friends as "Miss Sally" or "Uncle Joe" and this is just a respectful way of children's addressing adults without saying "Mr." or "Mrs."

When serving food, serve from the left and remove from the right. Water and wine are served on the right.

Who can give a shower? Actually, anyone who wants to give a shower for the bride may do so, except the immediate family. Mothers, mothers-in-law, sisters, etc. should *not*, under ordinary circumstances, give showers to honor other family members. A family member may inspire someone to give a party by saying, "I will help with the refreshments if you will host it." It is very inappropriate for someone related to the honoree to say, "Come give my daughter/sister a gift."

No one who is not invited to the wedding should be invited to a shower. If you are invited to a shower and do not get the invitation to the wedding, you might assume that it has been lost in the mail. Of course, the exception is the very small wedding with the guests being invited to the reception only.

There are rather specific rules about shower gifts. The gift is presented to the guest of honor at the shower. It is never sent to her from a store. If the donor cannot attend, she leaves the wrapped package at the hostess' house ahead of time. It must be accompanied by a card so that the guest of honor will know who gave the gift. All presents must be opened at the shower and each donor thanked personally, then and there. Elizabeth Post says that the recipient may write thank-you notes later if she wishes, but it is not necessary, unless the donor was not present at the shower to receive her personal thanks.

When you are invited to a shower for someone whom you do not know, or know well, and you refuse the invitation, you do not need to send a gift. Of course, if the shower is small or if it is a close friend, you will want to send a gift.

A proxy shower is perfectly correct when the bride lives at a distance. Gifts may be brought unwrapped, the hostess provides the wrapping materials; and the guests display their gifts, and then wrap them. The hostess may offer a prize for the prettiest package. Then she puts them all together and mails them to the bride. Usually, at a proxy shower, a telephone call is made to the bride—a delight for all!

Emily Post defined etiquette in 1922 as, "Beneath its myriad rules the fundamental purpose of etiquette is to make the world a pleasanter place to live in and you a more pleasant person to live with." Now, why should that ever be out of date?

WORD STUDIES

The *doily*, or crocheted mat, is English in origin and is named for Thomas D'Oyly. He was a linen draper who traded at the public house in Covent Garden during the seventeenth century. His small linen mats were used under bottles and finger bowls. Today we have a crocheted version, but frequently use paper doilies as liners on trays, etc. This intricate art executed in paper is beautiful and can create a fresh, crisp look.

Upper crust comes from an era of banqueting halls and baronial castles. The nobility sat near the lord and master. As the great crusted meat pies were served, those closer to the lord and master got upper, flaky crust, while those down the table were apt to get the soggy under crust.

The word *tip*—To Insure Promptness—originates in the seventeenth century. The first coffee houses in England were meetings places for writers, artists, and other learned notables. Merchants also found them suitable places for transacting business. One of the most famous coffee houses of the day was owned by Edward Lloyd. He used to list ships for the interest of the underwriters who frequented the coffee house. Later, it became known as Lloyd's Royal Exchange; today, it is the world-renowned Lloyd's of London. To speed service, the manager placed a box on the wall of the coffee house, intended for the waiter who would hurry as he heard the coins drop. Thus, *tip* was born. Wouldn't it be interesting to share the history of this word with some of our waiters and waitresses today.

Best bib and tucker come from the seventeenth century. The bib served to keep the gentleman's clothes clean; the tucker, usually lace or muslin, was tucked in the neck of the lady's dress for the same purpose. Thus, if you were dressed in your best bib and tucker you were all ready for a fancy party. (History tells us that the knife was the only eating utensil used until well into the eighteenth century; so the bib and tucker were of real importance.)

Drunk as a lord originated during the time of King George III of England, when intoxication was the mark of a gentleman. Two- or three-bottle men were not uncommon in society at that time. So *drunk as a lord* was a very popular mark of distinction.

Talk turkey means serious talk today. It comes from early colonial days and meant essentially the same thing. It seems that a white man and a friendly Indian decided to share their day's hunt. They bagged three crows, two turkeys. The white man divided, giving the crows to the Indian, the turkeys to himself. The Indian complained, "You talk all turkey for you, only crow for Indian."

Coffee dates back to the third century when a herdsman noticed his goats becoming unusually lively after eating berries of a certain shrub. He tried the berries himself and had a pleasant lift. He told the abbot of a monastery of his discovery, and the abbot gave some to the monks, who customarily fell asleep during nightly prayers. In 800 A.D., they were used as food in parts of Africa (ground up and mixed with grease and rolled into balls). Later, the custom of drying and roasting the berries spread to Arabia and to Europe. By the seventeenth century, Turkish invaders of Western Europe were driven off their land and they left behind large amounts of coffee. A Viennese secured enough to open a coffee house in Vienna where coffee was served as we know it today. From Vienna it traveled to Rome, where it became one of the most popular drinks in Italy. Today, America is the largest importer of coffee.

Drink a toast began in Shakespeare's time when a piece of toasted bread was put in the tankard before the ale or wine was poured. This was done to improve the taste, but more importantly, to collect sediment and impurities at the bottom of the vessel. Thus, the drink became a *toast*. *Toast of the town* is one who was very popular and caused many to drink to his or her health.

IN CLOSING

Many things have been said in these pages about entertaining, and you could tell me some things. But, the most important ingredient is "Not *what's* on the table . . . but *who's* in the chairs." (This is not original with me, but I can't remember who said it.)

Do invite your friends into your home! Life does become hectic, and it is so easy to "put it off." Disbanding the old neighborhood club is becoming a common occurrence. But, don't follow this style—don't even consider dissolving the Tuesday bridge group you have had for fifteen years. The circumstances of our lives, of course, dictate change, but it is so important that we keep in touch with friends. Call today and say, "Bring a salad and come to my house Saturday. I will prepare the drink and fresh fruit for dessert." (Everyone diets!) Then you surprise them with your yummiest, chocolate dessert; they'll love it!

The ingredients for contented living are faith, relationships (family and friends), experiences (the stuff memories are made of), and things—in that order. When my husband Jack and I were newlyweds this order was reversed. We knew we would always have family, and we thought that good ole Jane and Dick were good friends, but could be replaced by newer, more exciting people.

Later in life, a crisis comes. Jane and Dick are right there, and we realize they are not replaceable. They have sustained us when new friends could not. Then we lose a parent, or an Uncle Joe, and we realize families are not for always. We recall our happy experiences with our families, and realize these memories make difficult days easier.

Finally, we are truly adults and we realize "things" are not so important. Do we possess things or do things possess us? It's easy for possessions to become master. Those of you with silver in your hair (under the rinse of Loving Care) will nod in agreement from your own experience.

This book was written primarily as a help to all homemakers—things your mother would tell you if she were by your side. I almost wish you could have read this book back to front, as the Japanese do, for the message of this chapter is the fine thread that forms the theme of the designs I have tried to weave as I write this book.

I have never spoken to a group when I did not close with the comment that I would like each person to come to my home. And, my closing comment is always, "When God's children are in need, you be the one to help them out. And get into the habit of inviting guests home for dinner or, if they need lodging, for the night." (Romans 12:13, *The Living Bible.*)

In Closing

IT'S DELICIOUS . . .
THE EASY WAY
FAVORITE MENUS AND RECIPES

Meal planning can be a chore or it can be fun. There are thousands of cookbooks on the market. Yet we tend to use the recipes of our friends or those that we have enjoyed in someone else's home. Keep in mind these basic suggestions:

Plan ahead and try to prepare a large portion of one food that can be served in different ways throughout the week. Consider time and money.

In-season foods are good and inexpensive. When strawberries are "in," have as many different strawberry creations as you can master.

Do consider color. Someone has said that the eye eats first. Broiled chicken, squash souffle, rice, and a pear salad might be delicious to Grandmother with poor eyesight, but our eyes would crave a bit of color. Color is as important to the palate as to the plate.

With your entree you should have one vegetable (green or yellow), one starch, such as rice, potatoes, pasta, or corn, and a salad. (If you have growing boys you may want to have extras or extenders in the starch group.) Young hostesses usually overdo. If you have a filling meal, a light dessert is perfect. A lighter meal demands a heavy dessert.

That container of parsley in the refrigerator can add wonders to an otherwise drab meal. Use garnishes that you have on hand, such as grated hard-boiled egg yolks, crumbled bacon, or a touch of paprika. Many entrees need only a hearty salad and dessert to complete the menu. With chili, you would have salad, cobbler, and crackers. If your main course is spaghetti or vermicelli or lasagna, you might have tossed salad, bread sticks, and ice cream and cookies, or another simple dessert.

When you ask a mother to name her favorite child, it is an impossible request. So it is with my favorite menus and recipes. These are my favorite easy recipes. If recipes are too detailed and too long, they become a chore and not "Fun to Entertain."

OVEN MENU

PORK CHOPS WITH APPLES
CORN PUDDING
ESCALLOPED ZUCCHINI
GREEN SALAD
TOASTED POUND CAKE WITH ICE CREAM

When I serve this menu my guests leave their coats on when they come. There is nothing on the stove and they think we are going out to dinner!

Favorite Menus and Recipes

I did not drive for many years, and my husband traveled a great deal, so a lot of times I had to prepare meals with whatever I had on hand since I had no way to run to the grocery store. This pork chop recipe was created in just such an instance. I had guests coming for dinner and I had to put together a meal from whatever I had in my pantry.

PORK CHOPS WITH APPLES

Brown pork chops well on both sides; season with salt, pepper and cinnamon. Core, but do not peel, apples; line bottom of casserole dish with sliced apples. Place chops on top of apples, cover with more apple slices, and seal tightly with foil wrap.

Bake at 350° for about an hour. Baked apples are very tasty but do not have much eye appeal. Be sure to garnish this dish with spiced apple rings that come in a jar.

CORN PUDDING

2 cups corn (fresh or canned)	*2 eggs, beaten*
1 teaspoon sugar	*1 cup milk*
1 teaspoon vanilla	*1 tablespoon butter*
1 teaspoon salt	*2 tablespoons cracker crumbs*
¼ teaspoon pepper	

Use niblet or whole kernel corn, drained. Mix all ingredients together and pour into large casserole dish. Place casserole in hot water and bake 60 to 70 minutes at 350°. Yield: 6 to 8 servings.

ESCALLOPED ZUCCHINI SQUASH

6 small zucchini squash, cut in ¼ inch slices
½ teaspoon salt
½ cup sour cream
1 egg, beaten
⅔ cup Italian-type grated cheese
minced fresh green onion
MSG

Cook zucchini in little bit of salted water for just a few minutes—don't overcook. They should still be firm and a little crunchy. Drain *well* and place in casserole. Add beaten egg to sour cream; blend in little more salt, pepper, MSG, minced onion, and ½ of the grated cheese. Mix well and pour over squash, add rest of cheese on top, and bake at 400° for about 20 minutes, or until nice and bubbly. Yield: 6 servings.

BRUNCH MENU

MIMOSA
CHEESE STRATA
or EGG CASSEROLE
BAKED SOUTHERN GRITS
BAKED FRUIT
GRILLED TOMATO FLORENTINE
PUMPKIN BREAD
COFFEE

This Brunch Menu can be prepared a day in advance, except for the grits. Do remember to set out the Strata at least thirty minutes before it should begin cooking. I forgot once (only once!) and popped the cold dish into the hot oven. That was the innovation of scrambled eggs in Easy Toast Muffins. My guests continued to enjoy the Mimosa far longer than I had planned while I salvaged what I could of the Strata. After the casserole dish broke, I could not continue cooking in the oven, so there was quite a bit of improvising to complete that meal!

The Baked Fruit recipe originally had curry in it, but I found that my guests seem to enjoy the spice-sherry flavor even more.

MIMOSA APPETIZER
½ orange juice and ½ pink champagne. Garnish with fresh strawberry; serve in large bowl stem.

CHEESE STRATA *(can be made night before)*

3 eggs, beaten slightly	¼ teaspoon pepper
1½ cups milk	¼ teaspoon Worcestershire sauce
½ teaspoon brown sugar	¼ teaspoon red pepper
⅛ teaspoon paprika	soft butter or margarine
1 small onion, minced	4 slices bread
¼ teaspoon dry mustard	¾ pound shredded cheddar
¼ teaspoon salt	cheese

Combine eggs, milk, brown sugar, paprika, onion, mustard, salt, pepper, Worcestershire sauce, and red pepper. Set aside. Butter bread and cube. Put a layer of bread squares in baking dish, top with shredded cheese and repeat until all bread and cheese are used. Pour egg and milk mixture over all. Cover and refrigerate overnight. Take out 30 minutes before time for cooking. Bake at 300° for 1 hour. Just add extra cheese and eggs and milk if needed. You may add cooked bacon or sausage, if you want a complete meal in one dish. Yield: 8 servings.

An alternative could be an *Egg Casserole*, and it will be a good way to use up Easter eggs.

Slice 6-9 hard boiled eggs and place in a 11 x 14 casserole. Sprinkle with salt and pepper. Cook bulk sausage, drain well, and cover eggs. Spread over this a carton of sour cream, then about a cup of grated Cheddar Cheese on top. Cook about 25 minutes at 350°. Easy! Easy! The quantities are not too important. Use whatever quantity of eggs you want, cover generously with cooked sausage, sour cream and cheese. Garnish with parsley or pimento.

BAKED SOUTHERN GRITS *(prepare morning of party)*

1 teaspoon salt	1 cup milk
4 cups water	4 eggs, slightly beaten
1 cup hominy grits	½ cup shredded cheddar cheese
½ cup butter or margarine	

Add salt to water and bring to boil; stir in grits slowly, keeping water at a brisk boil. Cover and cook slowly for 1 hour, or until grits are soft, stirring occasionally. Remove from heat; stir in butter and milk. Cool to lukewarm; beat in eggs and turn into 2-quart casserole. Bake at 350° for 1 hour or until knife inserted in center comes out clean. Ten minutes before dish is done, sprinkle cheese over top and bake until golden brown. For more cheese flavor, add up to 1⅓ cup grated cheese before baking. Yield: 6 servings.

BAKED FRUIT *(Prepare day before party)*

1 1-pound can pear halves	12 maraschino cherries
1 1-pound can cling peaches	¾ cup light brown sugar
1 1-pound can pineapple chunks	3 teaspoons cinnamon
1 1-pound can apricot halves	3 teaspoons cloves
⅓ cup butter or margarine, melted	
⅔ cup blanched, slivered almonds	
sherry	

Drain all fruit. Add sugar and spices to melted butter. Arrange fruit and nuts in casserole; pour butter mixture over fruit, and add sherry. Bake an hour at 325°. Refrigerate overnight. Reheat at 350° before serving. Yield: 10 to 12 servings.

GRILLED TOMATO FLORENTINE *(cook spinach and prepare tomatoes day before)*

8 firm medium tomatoes
salt and pepper
butter
1 10-ounce package frozen spinach

Cook spinach according to directions on package; puree in blender. Cut off tops of tomatoes and season with salt and pepper. Place tomatoes in muffin tins; bake for 10 minutes at 350° or until heated through. Add spinach on top. Yield: 6 to 8 servings.

PUMPKIN BREAD *(can be done ahead of time) Makes one to use, one to freeze, one to share.*

1 teaspoon nutmeg	1 can pumpkin
1 teaspoon cinnamon	⅔ cup water
3 cups sugar	2 teaspoons soda
1 cup cooking oil	3 cups flour
4 eggs	1½ teaspoons salt
1 cup nuts	

Favorite Menus and Recipes

Beat together nutmeg, cinnamon, sugar, oil, eggs and salt. Add and mix in order: pumpkin, water, soda, nuts and flour. Grease well three 1-pound coffee cans, or 2 regular loaf pans; fill each half (plus a little) or equally full. Bake at 350° for about an hour. Let cool for 10 minutes, turn out and cool on rack.

LUNCHEON MENU

CHICKEN SALAD WITH WHITE GRAPES or
HOT CHICKEN SALAD
FROZEN CRANBERRY FRUIT SALAD
CHEESE BISCUITS
MARINATED ASPARAGUS OR GREEN BEANS
PARFAIT

I use a cold chicken salad in warmer weather, but it can be changed to a hot chicken salad for the winter months. Pecans can be used in the cold chicken salad, and I usually garnish either dish with grapes. (The red seedless grapes make a lovely plate.) Other frozen salads are included in these recipes, so you can select the one you prefer. This menu can also be prepared the day before. I even make the salad a week ahead of time.

CHICKEN SALAD

2 cups diced chicken   *1 cup chopped celery*
1 cup seedless grapes   *¼ cup mayonnaise*
¼ cup whipped topping

Toss chicken with remainder of ingredients, garnish with toasted, slivered almonds. (Be careful toasting almonds—they burn so easily.) Yield: 4-6 servings.

HOT CHICKEN SALAD

3 cups cooked chicken, diced
1½ cups celery, chopped
¾ cup slivered almonds
1 6-ounce can sliced water
  chestnuts
½ teaspoon salt
¾ cup grated sharp cheese

2 teaspoons grated onion
3 tablespoons lemon juice
1½ cups mayonnaise
1 11-ounce can cream of chicken
soup
1½ cups crushed potato chips

Combine everything except the cheese and potato chips in a greased 9-× 13-inch dish. Combine cheese and chips, then sprinkle on top. Bake at 325° for 45 minutes, until lightly brown. Yield: 8 servings. This is also a great recipe for a buffet.

FROZEN CRANBERRY FRUIT SALAD

2 3-ounce packages cream cheese
2 tablespoons sugar
2 tablespoons mayonnaise
1 1-pound can cranberry sauce, whole-berry
1 cup drained, crushed pineapple
½ cup chopped pecans
½ cup whipped topping

Cream together cheese and sugar; stir in mayonnaise. Fold in cranberry sauce, pineapple, nuts and whipped topping. Pour into baking cups in a muffin tin and freeze until firm. When they are firmly frozen, transfer them to plastic bag and keep in freezer until ready to use. When serving, remove cups and invert on lettuce bed on plate. Yield: 10-12 servings.

CHEESE BISCUITS

If you make homemade biscuits, add grated cheese to dough before rolling and cutting. But, if you don't have time to make biscuits from scratch, sprinkle cheese on cresent rolls, roll and bake; or, split in half canned biscuits, sprinkle cheese, replace top, and bake. Serve hot.

MARINATED ASPARAGUS

Place asparagus spears in shallow dish. Cover with Italian dressing and marinate overnight. Serve on luncheon plate and garnish with pimento.

Favorite Menus and Recipes

Whole green beans, canned or frozen, can be used instead of asparagus. The canned ones are so easy: drain and marinate. (They are cheaper, too!)

PARFAITS *(use parfait glasses or saucer champagne glasses)*
In the winter I like to alternate layers of creme de menthe liqueur and chocolate syrup with vanilla ice cream; garnish with cherries or nuts; serve with plain cookies, pound cake strips, or a tray of homemade cookies for the holidays.

For summertime, fresh strawberries with strawberry ice cream is nice; or fresh peaches with peach ice cream; or my favorite one, blueberries and mashed bananas with a dash of lemon juice over vanilla ice cream. So good and so lovely.

DINNER MENU

LONDON BROIL
POTATO CASSEROLE
ORANGE SALAD
OFF-BEAT CARROTS
COCONUT CHESS PIE

Now is the time to invite your husband to share the chores. The London Broil is excellent cooked on the grill (but it can be broiled in the oven), and husbands are such good cooks at the grill.

LONDON BROIL *or Flank Steak*
Marinate steak (recipe below) about 24 hours, turning occasionally.

Cook on grill, slice on bias, place on hot platter; pour mushroom mixture over top and garnish with parsley and whole mushrooms. Provide ¼ pound meat per person.

MEAT MARINADE

¾ cup soy sauce	2½ teaspoons lemon juice
1 tablespoon Worcestershire	3 teaspoons salt
1 stick margarine	3 teaspoons pepper
¾ teaspoon garlic salt	¾ teaspoon Tabasco

Warm margarine and mix remaining ingredients. Prick meat, pour marinade over meat and leave at room temperature for 2 to 3 hours. Refrigerate.

MUSHROOM SAUCE

1 pound fresh mushrooms
2-3 fresh green onions or scallions, finely minced
1 tablespoon butter
chopped parsley
½ cup wine

Slice mushrooms; melt butter and add remainder of ingredients. Simmer over low heat about five or ten minutes

POTATO CASSEROLE

1 32-ounce package frozen hash-brown potatoes (thawed)
1 can cream of chicken soup
1 8-ounce carton sour cream
2 tablespoons onion flakes
12 ounces grated sharp cheese
1 teaspoon salt

Mix together and pour into large, flat casserole. Crush two cups corn flakes and mix with ½ cup melted butter. Crumble this over the potato mixture. Bake at 350° for 30 minutes, covered; then bake 15 minutes, uncovered. Yield: 10 to 12 servings.

I always prepare salad fixings early so that at the last minute I only need to "put together" a salad to serve. Wash greens and any other fresh vegetables or fruits and drain on paper towels; store in refrigerator in plastic bags.

Favorite Menus and Recipes

There is a commercial sweet-sour dressing on the grocer's shelves now that is very nice, but I felt I needed to share a homemade dressing for you scratch cooks.

ORANGE SALAD

12 cups assorted greens
2 cups fresh orange sections (can use canned Mandarin orange sections)
6 green onions, thinly sliced
2 tablespoons chopped parsley
1 cup slivered almonds (reserve some to sprinkle on top)

Place all ingredients in large bowl, toss with sweet-sour dressing (below). Yield: 10-12 servings.

SWEET-SOUR DRESSING (for Orange Salad)

Blend all ingredients together and refrigerate at least 20 minutes before serving:

1 cup vegetable oil	½ cup white wine or tarragon
3 teaspoons sugar	vinegar
½ teaspoon salt	1 teaspoon tarragon
dash hot pepper	½ teaspoon pepper

This carrot recipe is a little different and very good. It is a favorite of one of my Richmond friends. Even those who dislike carrots enjoy Off-Beats.

OFF-BEAT CARROTS

Pare and dice 6 medium carrots; cook and drain. Place in buttered baking dish and cover with this mixture: ½ cup mayonnaise, 2 tablespoons onion (or onion salt), 2 tablespoons horseradish, ½ teaspoon salt and a dash of pepper. Top with ½ cup buttered breadcrumbs. Bake at 300° for 15-20 minutes. Yield: 6-8 servings.

This is "Blackie's Pie"! I have made this pie for 25 years—since a Richmond friend shared it with me—have taken it to covered dish suppers, to friends who were sick or grieved, and have contributed it as "a dessert for your party." I have given away this pie many, many times, but the recipe has been a family secret with me and my daughter, Suzanne. Now I want to share it with you. Enjoy!

COCONUT CHESS PIE

2 eggs, well beaten	¾ stick melted butter
1 cup sugar	1 can coconut
2 tablespoons sifted flour	1 teaspoon vanilla
dash of salt	1¼ cup milk

Add sugar to well beaten eggs; stir in flour and salt. Add remaining ingredients and stir until blended. Pour pie mixture into unbaked pie shell (9-inch). Bake at 425° for ten minutes; lower heat to 375° for thirty more minutes.

BUFFET MENU

BEEF TIPS IN WINE

RICE

EASY SPINACH or

GREEN BEANS WITH WATER CHESTNUTS

BEET SALAD

CHOCOLATE DELIGHT

The Beef Tips in Wine is a perfect recipe for your chafing dish and is so-o-o economical. I personally like the Green Beans with this menu, but if you are pressed for time, the Easy Spinach is nice.

As you can see, I have shied away from congealed salads. I hate the anxious moments of "will it come out?" This recipe is so colorful and delicious. Unmold the salad before you get in a rush, place it on the serving plate, garnish, and refrigerate until serving time.

Favorite Menus and Recipes

BEEF TIPS IN WINE

3 pounds chuck or round steak,
cut in 1½-inch cubes
¼ cup margarine
1 tablespoon flour
1 teaspoon salt
¼ teaspoon pepper

1½ cups Burgundy wine
3 medium onions, sliced
½ teaspoon thyme
½ teaspoon oregano
1½ cups beef broth
1 pound fresh mushrooms

Saute onions in margarine in heavy skillet or dutch oven. Brown meat on all sides with onions and margarine. Add flour and seasonings; stir until smooth. Add wine and broth; simmer 2 hours. Add mushrooms and cook another hour. Add wine and broth as it cooks. Put in chafing dish to serve over rice. (May be prepared ahead of time, reheated to serve.) Yield: 6-8 servings.

EASY SPINACH

2 packages frozen spinach, cooked and drained
1 carton sour cream
1 package dry onion soup mix

Cook spinach and drain well; add sour cream and onion mix; blend well. Cook in casserole dish about 20 minutes at 350°. Yield: 10-12 servings.

An alternative green vegetable is Green Beans With Water Chestnuts

3 10-ounce packages frozen French style green beans
½ cup butter
2 5-ounce cans water chestnuts, drained and sliced
salt and pepper to taste
3 tablespoons lemon juice
1 tablespoon soy sauce
sour cream to taste (optional)

Cook beans according to package directions; drain. In a skillet, heat butter and water chestnuts; stir in seasonings and add green beans. (Optional: at this point you can stir in some sour cream.) Pour into serving dish and garnish. Yield: 10-12 servings.

BEET SALAD

¾ cup celery, diced
1 cup diced beets (canned or cooked)
1 3-ounce package lemon gelatin
1 cup boiling water
¾ cup beet juice
2 tablespoons vinegar
½ teaspoon salt
2 teaspoons grated onion
1 teaspoon horseradish

Prepare celery and beets; set aside. Dissolve gelatin in boiling water; add beet juice, vinegar, salt, onion and horseradish. Chill until mixture is thick. Fold in beets and celery. Place in greased mold and chill. For a buffet, use a large mold on platter with a bed of lettuce. May serve with mayonnaise or sour cream. Yield: 8 servings.

This dessert can be made a week ahead of time. It is very rich, so cut the serving pieces into small squares and serve with a different kind of coffee, something exotic.

CHOCOLATE DELIGHT

22 Oreo Cookies, crushed
½ cup melted butter
1 quart coffee ice cream
2 small cans evaporated milk
nuts
3 blocks unsweetened chocolate
1 cup sugar
2 tablespoons butter
whipped topping

Mix melted butter with cookie crumbs, press out in long pyrex dish, and freeze. Cover with 1 quart coffee ice cream; freeze.

Cook together until thick: chocolate, sugar, 2 tablespoons butter, and evaporated milk. Cool; pour over ice cream. Cover with whipped topping, nuts and shaved chocolate, and return to freezer. Cut into squares to serve. Yield: 12-14 servings.

*   *   *

A Fish Mold is as good as it is pretty. It is as nice for a buffet, luncheon, or dinner party as it is for an hor d'oeuvre.

FISH MOLD

1 can mushroom soup
1 package plain gelatin, dissolved in 3 tablespoons water

Warm soup, add dissolved gelatin, and add the following:

6 ounces cream cheese
1 green onion, chopped fine
1 7-ounce can crab meat
1 cup chopped celery
1 cup mayonnaise
2 tablespoons sherry
½ teaspoon lemon pepper
½ teaspoon Accent
½ teaspoon Worcestershire sauce

Pour into fish mold and chill until firm. Unmold and use an olive for his eye. Serve with crackers or party-size breads.

*　　*　　*

Now tell me, what can be easier than this?

EASY APPETIZER

2 packages frozen Brussels sprouts
1 bottle Italian dressing
1 teaspoon dillweed

Cook Brussels sprouts according to package directions, drain. Chop dillweed and add with dressing to sprouts. Refrigerate at least 24 hours. Serve as appetizers with picks.

*　　*　　*

Put a package of frozen mixed fruit on your grocery list and you will always have a dessert on hand. The sour cream and brown sugar really does something to the flavor.

FROSTY FRUIT DESSERT

1 10-ounce package frozen mixed fruit
2 sliced bananas
¼ cup commercial sour cream
2 tablespoons brown sugar

Thaw fruit and add sliced bananas; chill. Spoon into footed stem; add generous spoonful of sour cream and sprinkle with brown sugar. Makes a delightful quick dessert. Can be accompanied by plain cookies, if desired.

*　　*　　*

Here are two more frozen salads. These can be frozen in pans or molds. I prefer to use muffin tins with cups. You have perfect serving quantities for luncheons or dinners. What a joy it is to have your salad made when you begin to select your menu.

FROZEN SALAD

4 bananas, mashed
1 8-ounce can crushed pineapple, drained
1 tablespoon lemon juice
1 6-ounce jar red cherries (drained, cut in fourths)
1 cup chopped pecans
¾ cup sugar
1 teaspoon salt
2 8-ounce cartons sour cream

Mix all ingredients together and freeze. Can be frozen in flat pan and cut into individual pieces; or frozen in baking cups and stored in plastic bag.

FROZEN WALDORF SALAD

1 8-ounce can crushed pine-apple	Drain, reserve juice; Add water to make ½ cup juice
2 eggs, beaten ½ cup sugar ⅛ teaspoon salt ¼ cup lemon juice	Combine in sauce pan with juice mixture; cook over medium heat until thick. Cool.
½ cup chopped celery 2 medium apples, chopped ½ cup chopped walnuts	Add to above mixture.
2 cups whipped topping	Fold into above mixture and freeze.

Do you have a crystal bowl? Layer fresh fruits and serve with this easy fruit dressing. It is perfect for *any* meal. I use any and all fruits in season. (Try to freeze a few blueberries for later.) Blueberries are my "garnish" on my fresh fruit bowl.

EASY FRESH FRUIT DRESSING

⅓ *cup frozen lemonade, undiluted*
⅓ *cup honey*
⅓ *cup oil*

Blend in blender. Add poppy seed or celery seed; store in refrigerator.

* * *

For you who never mastered the art of pie crust, here is Your Pie! It's perfect for the chocolate lovers.

NO-CRUST CHOCOLATE PIE

1¾ *cups sugar*	2 *eggs, beaten*
4½ *tablespoons cocoa*	1 *teaspoon vanilla*
2 *tablespoons flour*	1 *can evaporated milk*
¾ *stick melted butter*	

Mix ingredients in order given. Pour into 8- or 9-inch pie pan. Bake 30 to 50 minutes at 375°. Use nuts to garnish, or put them in batter.

* * *

Chicken Divan is an old, tried-and-true recipe. My friend, whose recipe I am sharing, said her family knows she can serve a regiment with one chicken when she uses this recipe!

CHICKEN DIVAN

1 *fryer, stewed,* cut into bite size pieces*
2 *packages frozen, chopped broccoli*
2 *cans cream of chicken soup*
1 *teaspoon lemon juice*
1 *cup mayonnaise*
½ *teaspoon curry powder*
½ *cup grated sharp cheese*
½ *cup bread crumbs*
1 *tablespoon butter*
pimento (optional)

Cook and drain broccoli, place in casserole. Place chicken pieces on top of broccoli. Combine soup, mayonnaise, juice, curry powder, and cheese. Pour over chicken. Sprinkle bread crumbs over top and dot with butter. Garnish with pimento. Bake 350° for 25 to 30 minutes. May be made ahead of time and frozen. Yield: 6-8 servings.

*Save chicken broth to cook rice, which goes well with this recipe.

* * *

This potato salad is a bit different from most potato salads. It is perfect with ham for a picnic or buffet.

DEVILED POTATO SALAD

6 hard-boiled eggs	2 tablespoons vinegar
6 medium potatoes, cooked	½ tablespoon horseradish
and cubed	2½ tablespoons mustard
1 cup chopped celery	½ teaspoon celery salt
1 cup sour cream	½ teaspoon salt
1 cup mayonnaise	

Mash and blend yolks with vinegar, horseradish and mustard. Add mayonnaise, sour cream, and salts. Mix well. Chop egg whites; combine with potatoes and chopped vegetables. Fold in egg mixture. Chill.

* * *

This next recipe can be made a week ahead of time. It is a most versatile vegetable dish that you can prepare when you are having house guests. Serve it the first time as a vegetable; later, use some of the marinade and a few carrots on slices of tomatoes for a "second salad." The carrots, drained, can be used for a garnish for meat.

MARINATED CARROTS

1 can tomato soup	1 teaspoon prepared mustard
½ cup oil	1 teaspoon Worcestershire sauce
1 cup sugar	salt
¾ cup vinegar	pepper

Mix together all of the above. Slice and boil 2 bunches of carrots in salt water until tender. Drain and cool. Alternate in bowl with onion slices; pour mixture over carrots and onions; refrigerate. Drain to serve. Yield: 10-12 servings.

*　　*　　*

For a simple dessert, or for hors d'oeuvres, serve seedless grapes in small bunches, apple and pear slices with cheese and crackers. Dieters and diabetics will appreciate these natural foods, and it is such a good combination.

GARNISHES

I have mentioned garnishing various dishes. Eye appeal is so important to food enjoyment—I garnish everything! Also, if you garnish in portions, it helps you know how many servings you can get out of a dish.

Parsley is the old standby garnish for meat or vegetables dishes. Fresh flowers are the perfect garnish for your sweet trays. Pull a single flower blossom through a lemon slice and see what a difference it makes on the tray.

Use a bunch of cheese carrots on a bed of parsley to garnish a canape tray or a sandwich tray. Make the carrots by hand, rolling any soft cheese into carrot shapes. Taper one end to a point; make a hole in the other end and prick with a toothpick. Insert parsley sprig to look like the carrot top. Use fork tines to make circular design around carrot. You will only need three or four carrots to garnish even a large tray.

Tomato roses are quick and easy. With a sharp knife, cut thin slice from top of tomato and discard. Begin at top and peel a paper-thin continuous strip about ¾ inches wide from the entire tomato. With the flesh side of the tomato peel inward, coil the strip tightly to form a rose. The last coil should be loose to form outer "petals."

Round radishes make perfect roses. Make petals by slicing down four sides almost to the bottom. Long radishes do nicely as accordians. Cut them along the long side, almost through to the bottom. Place either type in cold water to curl.

INDEX

Index